The Natural Soap Chef

The Natural Soap Chef

Making Luxurious Delights from
Cucumber Melon and Almond Cookie
to Chai Tea and Espresso Forte

HEIDI CORLEY BARTO

Ulysses Press

Published by:
Ulysses Press
P.O. Box 3440
Berkeley, CA 94703
www.ulyssespress.com

ISBN: 978-1-61243-062-1
Library of Congress Catalog Number 2012935761

Printed in China by Everbest Printing through Four Colour Print Group

10 9 8 7 6 5 4 3 2 1

Acquisitions editor: Keith Riegert
Managing editor: Claire Chun
Editor: Phyllis Elving
Proofreader: Lauren Harrison
Interior photographs: © Heidi Corley Barto except shutterstock.com images on page
    14 goggles © Picsfive, page 15 coffee and tea © Valentina_S, page 16 olive oil ©
    Angel Simon, page 17 shea butter © Elena Elisseeva, page 19 scale © spot-h, page
    19 stick blender © Melica
Cover photographs: © Heidi Corley Barto
Cover design: what!design @ whatweb.com

Distributed by Publishers Group West

To my husband Rick—
you're the cool whip to my cocoa!

CONTENTS

INTRODUCTION
ONE BAR AND I WAS HOOKED

I bought my first bar of handmade soap at a craft fair when my two girls were small. The woman at the craft fair told me she made it in her home, from oils, lye, milk, and plants she grew in her garden. I bought a bar because it smelled so delicious, and I thought it was fascinating that someone had actually made it. Then I used it and just fell in love. The bar seemed to last forever, and the lather was wonderful.

I needed to learn how to make soap! I ordered every book from my local library that mentioned soap making, and I looked online for whatever information I could find. I learned that there are different ways to make soap. One way is to melt and pour. You buy a soap base, melt it, add elements such as color, fragrance, and exfoliants, and then pour it into a mold. Another way is "rebatching." You shred existing soap, mix it with a liquid, and use that as your soap base. Both these methods are terrific ways to produce a quickly usable bar of soap, but they weren't what I wanted. I wanted to be able to make my own soap base and have total control over every ingredient.

I found what I was looking for with cold process soap making—the method Great Grandma used to made soap. She created soap from its basic components: lye + oil = soap. Great Grandma could be stirring that soap for days waiting for the necessary chemical reaction, but thanks to modern inventions such as the electric stick blender and the digital scale, the process is much faster and easier today!

> SAPONIFICATION—The chemical reaction that occurs when sodium hydroxide (lye), an alkali, meets a fatty acid (oil). The alkali splits the oil into two parts: a fatty acid and glycerin. The sodium joins with the fatty acid to form a sodium salt. Sodium salt is what we call bar soap.

Then I made some soap . . . and other things happened

After all my research, with the limited amount of information I'd been able to find, I attempted my first batch. I made some bars from lard and lye, with no fragrance, and thought I was pretty awesome. A couple of batches later, we were overrun with lardy-smelling bars of soap. Soap production ceased because we needed to use up the bars I'd already made. My husband, Rick, trooper that he is, helped me deplete my inventory of foul-smelling soaps.

Life happened. The company that Rick had been with for 17½ years closed. While Rick looked for work, I started a new job at the library where I'd checked out my soap-making books. We focused on raising our girls. Rick got a terrific new job, and I moved on to all sorts of different crafty endeavors. When I wanted to use homemade soap, I bought it from other soap makers.

Then Paige, my younger daughter, started to experience skin issues. I bought soap bar after soap bar, trying to find one that would help her dry, itchy skin. Then I had an epiphany: I would research different vegetable oils to see what each kind offered as far as benefits to the skin, and I'd make soap for Paige and my family. I asked my older daughter, Gillian, a chemistry student at the time, if she'd like to do an experiment in saponification with me. "Sure," she agreed, having no clue what the heck I was talking about. She'd been just a child when I'd last made soap.

We set out on our soaping adventure, leaving the lard alone and trying all sorts of vegetable oils instead. This time around, the resources were fantastic. There is so much support for soap makers, be it online or in print. I developed my own recipes and tailored them to my needs and the needs of my family. There were online soap calculators where I could plug in the types of oils I wanted to use and how much soap I wanted to make and learn what characteristics my soap would have. These tools helped me design a nice, hard bar that has great lather and is super moisturizing. Friends and family had fun testing my soap, and they've given me all sorts of ideas for new recipes to create.

Real soap

Many people like to limit the chemicals they use, and cold process soap making is an excellent way to do that. The "soap" that you buy in the grocery store usually isn't true soap. It's detergent, consisting primarily of synthetic ingredients. In addition, manufacturers usually strip their "soap" products of glycerin (a natural by-product of cold process soap making) to use in other products. Glycerin is a humectant, meaning that it attracts moisture. Cold process soap made at home still contains all of its natural glycerin. You'll notice a difference in how it moisturizes your skin.

Small batches

Handmade cold process soap can be made in your own kitchen, using items you probably already have and a few that you may want to buy. While many soap-making books have recipes that create 40-plus bars of soap, my recipes use just over a pound of oils and yield about eight 3½-ounce bars or six chunkier bars of about 4 ounces. This more modest use of ingredients keeps your soap-making costs within reason.

> A NOTE ON YIELD—
> Unless otherwise noted, all my recipes make about 20 ounces, enough for 8 standard bars or 6 chunkier bars, 3½ to 4 ounces each.

Smaller batches are also ideal for experimenting. For example, some friends asked me to make a roasted garlic soap. I agreed, but I told them that they'd be trying it out, not me! (Usually people use soap to get the food smells off their hands, not the other way around.) I'm still waiting for a review on that one. Considering the public's current obsession with vampires, I could probably find some teenage girls willing to take it off my hands.

If you can read this, you can make soap!

The step-by-step instructions in this book will have you making your own soap in no time. Impress your friends with words such as "saponification" and look hip in rubber gloves and goggles!

Soap making is not an enterprise to be taken lightly, however. Working with lye can be dangerous for someone who is unprepared. Lye is a caustic substance that can cause chemical burns, scarring, and blindness, or even be fatal if swallowed. You can safely double the recipes in this book, except those in Chapter 6, Recipes to Impress. However, working small and following all safety precautions will keep the risk to a minimum. Remember: Stay small and it's easier to stay safe.

All my recipes have been tested by me and have been run through a lye calculator to ensure that there will be no lye left in your finished bars of soap. Cold process soap does have a recommended cure time of four weeks, but a great bar is worth waiting for! The resulting bars of soap will be mild and produce a generous lather.

I'm hoping that this book will inspire the burgeoning soap maker within you to learn, create, experiment—and go off on your own soap-making adventure. I hope the photographs make you want to learn something new. I hope I've explained things in a way that makes soap making seem a lot less scary, and even fun. Soap making is a great hobby, and it's a wonderful way to be artistic and utilitarian at the same time. Use my recipes, create your own, just have fun. That's all I ask.

CHAPTER 1
SOAP-MAKING ESSENTIALS

"You can do it, I have faith in you!" — My Mom

In this chapter you'll learn about all the ingredients and equipment you'll need to make cold process soap, so read on!

All real soap starts with a little lye

Sodium hydroxide (NaOH)—what we commonly refer to as lye—is an alkaline substance that's the basis of any soap recipe. Lye can be purchased online from soap supply companies in the form of crystals, beads, or flakes. When buying online from a reputable company, you will be required to fill out a hazardous material waiver form to submit with your order.

Lye can also be purchased at some hardware stores, and I buy mine from my local tractor supply. The container may say "drain cleaner" or "drain opener." Look at the ingredients list—you want it to say 100% sodium hydroxide. If your local hardware store salesperson looks at you funny, it's because lye is also used in the production of crystal meth. Just let him know that you make soap!

Lye safety

Mixing lye with a liquid causes an exothermic chemical reaction. This means that lye will heat up any liquid to which it's added. A room-temperature liquid can heat up above 200°F with the addition of lye.

Always add the lye crystals to whatever you're using as your liquid. Never add liquid to your lye crystals! Adding liquid to the lye will cause a volcanic reaction—the surest way to get burned. This is a major no-no in soap making!

Always store your lye container tightly closed in a cool, dry place out of the way of animals and small children.

Ventilation

I make my soap right in my kitchen. My quantities are small, but I always take certain precautions. I make sure the kitchen is well ventilated, with my ceiling fan on. If you have windows in the room you're working in, open them a bit. Make sure the air is moving around.

When you add your lye to your liquid, never stand so that you're breathing directly over the container. Some liquids that you use may give off a strong odor. It's best to be in the habit of not inhaling directly above what you're mixing.

Rubber gloves and goggles

Chemical-resistant gloves and chemical goggles must be worn when measuring lye crystals, adding crystals to the liquid called for in a recipe, adding the lye mixture to the oil mixture, using a stick blender, and pouring soap into molds. If you're wondering when to wear them, just wear them!

Don't confuse chemical goggles with safety goggles. Safety goggles will not protect your eyes from liquids. Chemical goggles have clear plastic lenses and a rim that seals around your eyes. You can buy both the gloves and the goggles at a hardware or soap-making supply store. Bramble Berry (www.brambleberry.com) sells some really cute colored goggles that will protect your eyes and look fashionable.

Water, water, and more water

Even when you've observed safety precautions, you may splash your soap mixture. Be sure to be close to running water in case raw soap or your lye mixture gets onto your skin. Wipe off the spill with a paper towel, go to the sink, and rinse the area with lots of water. Rinsing for several minutes will help neutralize the lye before it burns you. If you splash soap in your eyes, remove any contact lenses and flush your eyes for about 20 minutes, then get medical attention—but none of that will happen because you'll be wearing your goggles!

Liquid Ingredients

Your lye crystals must be dissolved in a liquid before you can add it to your oils and butters to make soap. Many different types of liquids can be used, and each adds something to the finished bar of soap.

Distilled water

The only type of water used in this book's recipes is distilled water. You should always use pure water when making soap, and distilled water is free of minerals and contaminants. It's also readily available at any grocery store, alongside the spring water. I keep a gallon in my fridge.

Any recipe in this book that calls for goat's milk, coconut milk, beer, tea, or a purée can also be made using just distilled water, if that's what's available to you and you are just dying to get started.

Goat's milk

Goat's milk is just wonderful in soap, offering many benefits for your skin. It cleans and softens the skin without drying it, and it's perfect for sensitive skin. The acids in goat's milk help exfoliate and encourage cell turnover. The alkalinity of goat's milk is similar to that of your skin.

Coconut milk

Coconut milk adds a bubbly moisturizing lather to soap. You can find it at any grocery store, but don't confuse coconut milk with coconut cream. The can should say "milk." Also stay away from "light" coconut milk. We're making soap, not worrying about calories. Soapers like fat!

Tea and coffee

Tea made with distilled water and any flavor of tea bag or loose tea can be used in soap. The scent may not remain in the final bar of soap, but the tea can add color, and tea leaves will add texture.

The aroma of coffee, like that of tea, really doesn't make it through to the cured bar, but the color does. Brew strong coffee with distilled water; I use espresso or any boldly flavored coffee.

Beer and stout

Beer or stout in soap results in a bar that has terrific lather. Boiling for 5 minutes will remove the alcohol content; let it cool, and then chill until it's flat—you don't want any carbonation remaining. Adding lye to beer or stout gives off an awful smell, but don't worry, this odor won't be present in your bar of soap.

Purées

I like to experiment. Sometimes I use a purée to add color or lather to soap. I'll mix fresh fruit or vegetables with any of the liquids mentioned previously. An easy way to incorporate purées is to use baby food—no blender necessary.

Oils and butters

Every oil and butter used in making soap adds certain characteristics to the final product. They also have different values at which they'll saponify. This means that it takes different amounts of lye to turn each type of oil or butter into soap, which means you cannot substitute oils in a recipe.

Castor oil (liquid)

Extracted from the castor bean plant, this oil adds conditioning and creamy lather to soap. Include it in your soap recipe when you want big, thick, bubbly lather. I use it in my shampoo bar recipes. You don't need a lot to reap its benefits.

You can find castor oil in small quantities in the grocery store, sold as a laxative. A soap-making supply company will sell it in the larger amounts that you'll need for making soap.

Coconut oil (75°F melting point)

Cleansing and bubbly, coconut oil adds hardness to your bar of soap. Keep its use below 30% of the total oils used in the recipe unless your recipe calls for superfatting, or it could be drying to the skin.

Olive oil (liquid)

This oil produces a mild, conditioning soap. The lower grades of olive oil are excellent for making soap—don't use extra-virgin olive oil unless the recipe specifically calls for it.

Palm oil (solid at room temperature)

Palm oil contributes to bar hardness, conditioning, and creamy lather. Make sure your palm oil supplier supports sustainable palm oil production. The supplier will specify if it is a member of the Roundtable on Sustainable Palm Oil (RSPO), an organization that supports sustainable palm oil production.

Shea butter (solid at room temperature)

Very conditioning, shea butter yields creamy lather and adds to bar hardness. This solid butter will melt on contact with your skin.

Extras

Exfoliants

Many people like a bit of scrubbiness in their soap. Some of the exfoliants used in this book's recipes are oatmeal, tea leaves, coffee grounds, and ginger.

Essential oils and fragrance oils

Essential oils and fragrance oils can be purchased from any soap-making supply company. Many suppliers will tell you whether or not a fragrance works well in cold process soap. They should also tell you whether a fragrance will discolor the soap. Discoloring isn't a bad thing—it's a great way to produce colored soap without having to add artificial coloring.

The site from which I buy my fragrance provides a handy little online gadget called a fragrance calculator. You plug in what kind of soap you're making and how much, and select a fragrance. The calculator then tells you how much of the fragrance to use, depending on how strong you want the scent to be.

> PLEASE NOTE—All my recipes use essential and fragrance oils from Bramble Berry (www.brambleberry .com) so all the recipes in this book are formulated using their products. The formulas and concentrations of oils vary among manufacturers, so if you use a different brand, the amount you'll need to add and its effect on the color of the soap will vary as well.

Colorants

There are pigments that you can purchase to color soap, and any soap-making supply company will carry them. You can also use small amounts of spices and other natural ingredients, like mica and clay, to color soap. The soaps in this book are colored without the use of pigments. I do use clay in some recipes and spices in several. The spices I use are the same ones used for cooking and are available in your grocery store.

Clays

Clays add color and slip to your soap, and they also help absorb oil. I use bentonite clay in my shaving bars. Clays are available at any soap-making supply store or at a beauty supply store.

Soaping Hardware

Some of your soap-making equipment should be used only to make soap. Other items, once washed, are fine for other kitchen tasks as well. In this book, I use the notation (DTS)—Dedicate to Soap—for the things you should reserve for soap making only.

Don't go crazy buying new equipment for a hobby that you haven't even tried yet. You probably have usable items or duplicates kicking around in your cabinets, or your local thrift store is an excellent place to look for what you need. Also ask around. Tell your friends what you plan to do and the tools you'll need. Some of them may have an extra Pyrex pitcher or spare spatula they can give you. Tell them you'll give them a bar of soap as payment. People love free soap!

Soap molds (DTS)

Soap molds are available through any soap supplier, from inexpensive plastic molds to more expensive wooden ones. Before you buy a mold, check to see if you already have things in your kitchen that will work, such as plastic storage containers that are dishwasher/microwave safe. Just be sure to dedicate these to soap making, because any fragrances you use will leach into the plastic. What kid wants a sandwich that smells like lilacs?

Wooden molds (DTS)   I use a 2-pound wooden mold made of Baltic birch, put together with carriage bolts and wing nuts. Wooden molds are sturdier and more insulated than plastic molds, but unlike a plastic mold, a wooden mold needs to be lined. Use freezer paper with the shiny side facing out as a liner. Some companies sell reusable liners that fit their molds perfectly. Some molds come with a template that gives you the exact dimensions your liner should be.

I line each mold piece individually with freezer paper and fasten the paper to the wood with waterproof first-aid tape. Then I assemble the mold. The pieces are a tight fit, but this protects the wood, and there's no leaking. I reline the mold each time. I store my mold upside down in my freezer until I'm ready to use it.

Milk cartons (DTS) How about milk cartons? The perfect mold for a beginning soap maker is a paper milk carton. I prefer the quart size, but a half-gallon container works fine, too. Cut the top off the carton, right along the top edge. This gives you a nice vertical mold. Rinse and dry the carton and set it aside until you need it. I put mine upside down somewhere so it won't collect dust inside.

The best part of using a milk carton is that you can just tear it away when the soap is ready. If the seam lines from the carton annoy you, use freezer paper to line the carton. Or simply use a vegetable peeler to trim away the seams from the cured soap.

Plastic and silicone molds (DTS) These molds come in all shapes and sizes, from one-piece loaves to multi-piece 3D soap shapes. One-piece plastic molds can be very inexpensive, but I find them difficult to unmold. Silicone molds can be a bit flimsy for soap making, so be sure to look for ones with reinforced sides and bottoms.

Digital scale

Soap making requires that all measurements be done by weight, not by volume. The ratio of lye to oils is extremely crucial. Accurate measurements assure that there will be no reactive lye in your finished soap.

All oil, liquid, and sodium hydroxide (lye) measurements in this book are given in grams. I started making soap by measuring in ounces, but I found grams to be more accurate and easier to read on the scale. Your digital scale needs to show 1-gram weight increments. For the recipes in this book, a kitchen food scale is perfect. A tare function is a necessity, letting you place your empty container on the scale and zero out its weight so that you can measure only your ingredients. Even inexpensive scales have this function—just be sure to check before purchasing.

Stick blender (DTS)

You can stir your soap mixture by hand if you want, but sometimes it can take days! I recommend that you purchase an electric stick blender (sometimes called an immersion blender). It will make your soap making so much easier!

You can buy a stick blender wherever small appliances are sold. Mine cost less than $20, and I use it only for making soap. It doesn't need to be heavy duty; you're only mixing liquids. However, once you use it for soap, I recommend you don't use it for anything else.

Two thermometers

Temperature is terribly important in soap making, and you'll need two thermometers. I started making soap using both a glass-covered candy thermometer and a digital thermometer with a stainless steel probe. The glass one went into my oil mixture, the digital one into my lye mixture. Due to a dishwashing mishap that no one wants to take credit for, I've since upgraded to two digital thermometers.

Whichever type you can get your hands on will work. Just be sure the sensors on your thermometers are made of glass or stainless steel; lye reacts with certain metals, but stainless steel is fine. Once cleaned, your thermometers are safe to use for cooking.

Silicone spatulas (DTS)

These are important for mixing the lye mixture and soap mixture, for scraping soap into molds, and more.

Heat-safe glass container (DTS)

You'll need a heat-safe glass container for your lye mixture. One with a pour spout is preferable.

Small glass mixing bowls (DTS)

Bowls that hold about 1 cup (8 liquid ounces) are perfect for weighing fragrances and lye crystals.

Pipettes (DTS)

Similar to eye droppers, these thin plastic pipettes are used to transfer fragrance oils and essential oils from their bottles into your measuring bowl. Pipettes can be purchased in bulk from soap-making supply companies, pharmacies, and beauty supply stores.

Frosted-plastic container (DTS)

For mixing your soap, you'll need a 2-quart to 1-gallon plastic container that's freezer and dishwasher safe. Why frosted plastic? It's quieter than the clear type when you are using your stick blender!

Measuring spoons

Use these to measure add-ins such as exfoliants, honey, or tea leaves. Note: While plastic measuring spoons are fine for most add-ins, use metal ones to transfer fragrance—the fragrance will etch the plastic spoons.

Spray bottle of isopropyl alcohol

Alcohol is used to help prevent a white powdery substance from forming on your bars. Be sure to get isopropyl, not rubbing alcohol—the alcohol content in rubbing alcohol isn't high enough to do the job. I keep my alcohol in a little spray bottle that I purchased at the dollar store.

Lining paper (for wooden molds)

You'll find plastic-coated freezer paper at the grocery store near the plastic wrap and trash bags. This protects your wooden molds and makes unmolding a breeze.

Plastic wrap

Yep, this is the same plastic wrap you already have in your kitchen. It's used to protect the top of your soap while it's curing.

Saucepan/pot

This is used like a double boiler to melt butter and oils. It must be large enough to be able to fit your plastic container holding all of the measured oils and have room enough to add some hot water around that container.

Cutting tool

Many different tools will work for cutting your soap into bars. You can use a soap cutter—basically a dough scraper with a wooden handle. Just to

save time, I ended up buying a box-type wooden soap cutter that has a channel for the cutting blade. Perfect vertical slices every time!

You can use a kitchen knife, but don't use a thick one—the thickness will cause your soap to break instead of making a clean cut all the way through. Thin knives are not ideal, but they will work if that is all you have. Just have a slow, steady hand. Another option is wire. A wire cheese cutter will cut your soap, but it may leave little lines in the bar.

Here is a handy checklist of soaping hardware you can use to make sure you have all the tools you'll need before you get started:

- ❑ soap mold
- ❑ digital scale
- ❑ stick blender
- ❑ two thermometers
- ❑ silicone spatula
- ❑ heat-safe glass container
- ❑ small glass mixing bowls
- ❑ pipettes
- ❑ 2-quart to 1-gallon frosted plastic container
- ❑ measuring spoons
- ❑ spray bottle of isopropyl alcohol
- ❑ lining paper (if using wooden mold)
- ❑ saucepan
- ❑ cutting tool

CHAPTER 2
MY PROCESS, STEP BY STEP

Soap making may seem difficult, but it really isn't. You have your oil mixture on one side and your lye mixture on the other. You're either heating something up or cooling something down. When both mixtures get to the temperature called for in your recipe, you're ready to add your lye mixture to your oils. You blend them together, a chemical reaction starts, and the soap making begins. It's pretty straightforward, and with practice you'll be able to whip up a batch pretty quickly. Now for the step-by-step part...

Get your mold ready

I make sure the wooden mold I'm going to use is completely lined with freezer paper before I begin. The freezer paper should be shiny side out. This is the side that will touch your soap.

I always place my mold in my freezer, upside down, until I'm ready for it. Soap making creates some heat, and having a cold mold keeps your mixture from getting too hot.

Plastic molds or milk cartons should be clean and dry—you don't need to line or chill them. Chilling isn't necessary because they aren't as insulated as wood molds. I usually have them set off to the side somewhere, upside down, to prevent dust or debris from settling inside.

Read your recipe!

Are you using any liquids other than plain distilled water? If so, read the recipe to see if you need to do any extra prep work. Do it now before you continue with the process.

Measure your oils

For beginners—Glass bowls are perfect for measuring your oils and but-ters. Place the bowl on your digital scale and push the button that zeros out its weight. (That way you'll be weighing the contents, not your container.) Measure your first oil, then use a silicone spatula to transfer it from the bowl into your plastic mixing container. Repeat this process for each oil or butter in your recipe.

For the more experienced—If you feel comfortable measuring directly into your plastic mixing container, place it on your digital scale and reset the weight to zero. Begin adding your oils. I usually start with the liquid oils. Zero out your scale after the addition of each oil. Pour very, very slowly. With your more solid oils, add just a little bit at a time. Go slowly! If you go a little over, use a spoon to scoop some out until your measurement is correct.

Heat the oils

Set your plastic mixing container containing the oils into a saucepan or other pot. Pour some hot tap water into the pan, just enough that the mix-

ing container begins to float. It shouldn't be floating around too much, just enough so it isn't sitting directly on the bottom of the pan.

Insert a thermometer into the oil. You may not even need to turn on your stove burner, depending on how warm the room is. If you do, only turn it as high as warm. You only want the solid oils to melt and the temperature to go as high as called for in your recipe. It may go higher than you need—just try to monitor it to make sure that it doesn't climb above 150°F.

Measure the lye and liquid

Put on your goggles and gloves! Leave them on for the rest of the soap-making process.

Place a glass container on your digital scale and zero out its weight. Using a spoon, measure your lye crystals into the container. Break up any

Measuring lye crystals *Adding lye crystals to liquid*

clumps with the spoon. Set the container where it's safely out of the way of pets and children. Put the spoon in your sink, into a container filled with soapy water. It's better to be safe and have a few more dishes to wash than to accidentally get lye crystals where they shouldn't be!

Set a heat-safe glass container on your digital scale and zero out its weight. Measure out the amount of liquid your recipe calls for.

Add the lye to the liquid

Depending on what liquid you're using, you may need to use an ice or cold water bath around your heat-safe glass container to keep the temperature down. Check the recipe.

Slowly add your lye crystals to your liquid, stirring with a silicone spatula and making sure all the crystals dissolve. Some crystals may want to stick to the bottom, so scrape the bottom of the container with your spatula.

Insert a thermometer into the lye mixture to monitor the temperature. (I use the kind with a digital readout and a stainless-steel probe.) The temperature can get very high—as much as 200°F for lye and distilled water mixtures. Mixtures with milk or a purée shouldn't be allowed to get too high, because they can burn. Use an ice or cold water bath around those to try to keep the temperature below 140°F.

Monitor your temperatures

You'll notice that each recipe includes a mixing temperature. This is the temperature that the oils and the lye mixture need to be in order to make

soap. It's a dance, trying to get your lye mixture and your oils to the same temperature at the same time. It may sound difficult, but it's really not, and it gets easier the more batches you make.

Always keep watch on your lye mixture. Once it gets close to the target temperature, it's easy to either heat up or cool down your oils. I have everything right on my kitchen counter next to the stove and sink. My saucepan is ready with hot water to bring temperatures up, and there's a container of ice water in the sink to bring temperatures down. Once both the lye mixture and the oils are at the right temperature, you're ready to create soap!

Get your mixture to trace

Take the mixtures out of their water baths, if you used them. You can now add the lye mixture to the oil mixture. Using a stick blender and a silicone spatula, blend for a couple of pulses. You'll notice that the mixture may start to thicken. When it starts to look like cake batter, then the chemical soap-making process is starting to occur. Lift your blender or spatula and drizzle some of the mixture across the surface. If it drizzles like pancake batter and leaves a faint trail that stays on top for a bit before sinking down, this is called a light "trace." You will notice in the soap recipes that some ingredients—fragrances or exfoliants, for example—are added at this stage.

Your mixture will become thicker the more you blend. You don't want it to get too thick, however. I use my stick blender until medium trace and then just stir with my spatula. Medium trace is like thick gravy, and drizzled trails will stay on the top. If you blend even

WHAT IS FALSE TRACE? When the temperature of your soap mixture falls below the melting point of any solid oil that you're using, your mixture will thicken as if it has reached trace—but it really hasn't. Your mixture must begin to trace in order for the soap-making to begin. To prevent a false trace, make sure the temperature of the mixture doesn't fall far below the mixing temperature called for in the recipe. If a false trace does occur, use a hot-water bath to bring the temperature back up and help melt the solid oils.

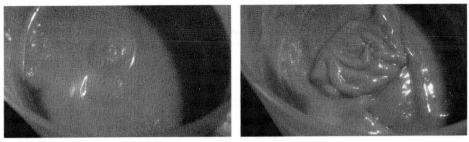

Light trace   *Medium trace*

longer, you'll achieve heavy trace, which is like a too-thick pudding, and you'll be able to make waves and designs that will stay without sinking.

Time to pour

When your soap mixture reaches medium trace, it's ready to pour. Carefully pour the mixture into the mold that you've selected. Use a silicone spatula to scrape any remaining soap mixture out of the container. Tap the sides of the mold gently to release any air bubbles. I usually lift the mold slightly and gently drop it down to get rid of any air bubbles at the bottom of the soap loaf.

Make the tops pretty

There are lots of ways to produce pretty tops for your soap. Pay attention to the way you pour your batter into the mold—you can make beautiful designs just by pouring or drizzling from your spatula. You can also use a plastic utensil to create swirls, little waves, or whatever looks good to you.

Let the soap set up for about 30 minutes, uncovered, in the refrigerator. Soap mixtures can get extremely hot, depending on the ingredients, and sometimes they can crack across the top. Keeping them cool can pre-

vent any cracking. Remove the soap from the refrigerator, spray the top with isopropyl alcohol, cover it loosely with plastic wrap, and refrigerate overnight. On soaps that contain honey, I use bubble wrap to make them look like honeycombs. I just cut a piece of bubble wrap—the kind with small bubbles—to fit the top, then press it down gently into the mixture. I don't remove the bubble wrap until it's time for the soap to come out of the mold. The bubble wrap keeps ash from forming, so there is no need for the isopropyl alcohol when bubble wrap is used.

Unmold your soap

Your soap only needs to refrigerate overnight. Then is sits in the mold at room temperature for at least 24 hours. If soap is made using only olive oil, I allow it sit for at least 48 hours. You may notice that your soap has pulled away from the sides of the mold. This is one sign that it's ready. If at any time while you're unmolding the soap seems too soft, set it aside and wait another day. Patience!

Wooden molds—Disassemble the mold, long sides first and then the end pieces. Twist the mold away from the soap, don't pull or peel, to keep from pulling the soap away, too. Finally, twist the bottom off and gently set the loaf aside on a protective surface. I have plastic cutting boards that I use for this.

Milk cartons—Unmolding soap from a milk carton is easy. Simply peel away at the carton until your soap is revealed!

Plastic and silicone molds—These can be tricky to unmold. The soap needs to be very hard in order to unmold without losing its shape. Some manufacturers recommend putting the molds in the freezer overnight. The soap should then pop out easily.

When you do unmold your soap, set it aside for a few minutes and let it rest and come to room temperature. If you had to freeze it, let it thaw completely.

Cut the bars

Your soap should always be at room temperature before you cut it. If it's too cold it will break, too hot it will mush. When I cut my soap, I lay the

loaf on its side and make my first cut close to the end, to see whether it's ready for cutting. If the soap mushes instead of holding its shape, the loaf is not ready! Leave it out again at room temperature for another try the following day.

When using your soap cutter or kitchen knife to cut your soap loaf, try your best to keep the slices vertical. I lightly spray my cut bars of soap with isopropyl alcohol again, and then it's off to cure!

Cure and store your soap

Cold process soap needs to cure for four to six weeks. Curing ensures that saponification is complete, that no lye is left in the soap, and that the resulting soap won't irritate your skin. During this curing time, any excess water evaporates from the bar, leaving a hard, long-lasting soap.

The best place to cure your soap is somewhere warm and dry. I've turned one of the most unused, junk-catching places in my home into something useful: The top of my fridge is now a soap-curing station. I have three ventilated shelves there where my soap bars go after I cut them. You can put different-scented soaps side by side, just don't let them touch each other. I leave them there for several weeks, until I need that space to cure new soap. Then I box them and store them somewhere out of the way.

If you don't have space to leave your soap out to cure, you can keep the bars in cardboard boxes. The soap will still be able to cure in the cardboard. I buy 10 x 4 x 4-inch corrugated cardboard mailers at my local office supply store. You can use a bigger box, but this size works for me. The ones I buy have flapped lids, but I purposely don't tuck in the flaps. The soap is still losing moisture, and I want to make sure it's able to breathe. These boxes can also be used for storing the soap once it has cured.

Never use plastic for storage—it doesn't breathe! You also don't want to store soaps with different fragrances in the same box. Short-term storage in the same box, like for gift-giving and shipping, is fine, but not for weeks at a time.

Clean up

Cleaning up is easy. Place all glass containers in a sink filled with water. Rinse, then wash by hand with dishwashing soap, or wash in your dishwasher. You can throw away fragrance pipettes or label them with the fragrances you used and continue to use them for those same fragrances.

I set my plastic container, spatula, and the removable end of my stick blender up out of the way, where no one will touch them, and let the soap mixture harden on them for several days. Then I soak them in a sink filled with hot water so that the soap dissolves. Once it has dissolved completely, I wash as usual.

This is the safest way to clean up. A raw liquid soap mixture is not a good thing to have in your pipes—it turns to a gel that can wreak havoc with plumbing. If you feel the need to wash right away, try to wipe most of the raw soap off with paper towels. Throw the paper towels in the trash.

CHAPTER 3
BEGINNER RECIPES

What really makes these recipes great for new soap makers is that they only use distilled water, rather than milks, teas, and other liquids. There is no special preparation for the distilled water other than having it chilled. Lye mixtures made with distilled water also have no maximum temperature, so monitoring the temperature is much easier.

BASIC OLIVE OIL SOAP

mix temp **110°F** *Bars made using just olive oil should be left in the mold for at least 48 hours. They will need at least 4 to 6 weeks to cure.*

You can add fragrance to this soap if you wish. Using an online fragrance calculator, select your fragrance and calculate for cold process soap at 20 ounces to determine how much to use.

FRAGRANCE-FREE

OIL

567 grams olive oil

LYE MIXTURE

73 grams sodium hydroxide (NaOH)

215 grams distilled water

1. Measure the olive oil into your plastic container. Place the container in a larger pot and pour in enough hot tap water that the container begins to float. Set the pot on the stove and turn the heat to warm. Insert a thermometer into the oil.

2. Goggles and gloves on!

3. Measure the water into a heat-safe glass container. Measure the lye crystals into a separate small glass container. Slowly add the lye crystals to the water, stirring with your spatula as you do so. Do not inhale above this container—there will be fumes that can take your breath away! This mixture will heat up quickly. Insert a thermometer into the mixture.

4. Monitor the temperatures of the two containers. Basically, you are heating up the oil while the lye cools down. You want both to reach 110°F. As needed, refresh the hot water bath or turn the stove burner higher to raise the temperature, or use a cold water or ice bath to bring the temperature down.

5. When both the oil and the lye mixture are at 110°F, pour the lye mixture into the plastic container with the oil. Blend with your stick blender until the mixture reaches medium trace (see page 26).

6. Pour into a chilled mold and refrigerate, uncovered, for 30 minutes. Remove from the refrigerator; spray the top with isopropyl alcohol, cover loosely with plastic wrap, and refrigerate overnight.

7. Remove from the refrigerator and let sit at room temperature.

8. Unmold 48 hours after pouring into the mold. Cut into bars and place in your curing area.

ROSEMARY OLIVE OIL SOAP

mix temp
110°F *This recipe can be made from items found at your grocery store. Rosemary is said to have many culinary and medicinal uses, but what I know for a fact is that it makes a delightful, fragrant soap. The bar has a light, fresh scent. You'll need to make the rosemary-infused oil the day before.*

FRAGRANCE-FREE

OILS

397 grams rosemary-infused olive oil (see directions below)

170 grams coconut oil

LYE MIXTURE

81 grams sodium hydroxide (NaOH)

215 grams distilled water

ADD AT TRACE

½ teaspoon chopped dried rosemary

1. Measure the oils and pour into your plastic container. Place the container in a larger pot and pour in enough hot tap water that the container begins to float. Set the pot on the stove and turn the heat to warm. Insert a thermometer into the oil.

2. Goggles and gloves on!

3. Measure the distilled water into a heat-safe glass container. Measure the lye crystals into a separate small glass container. Slowly add the lye crystals to the water, stirring with your spatula as you do so. Do not inhale above this container—there will be fumes. This mixture will heat up quickly. Insert a thermometer into the mixture.

4. Monitor the temperatures of the two containers. You want both to reach 110°F. As needed, refresh the hot water bath or turn the stove burner higher to raise the temperature, or use a cold water or ice bath to bring the temperature down.

Check Out Receipt

Linda Vista Library
858-573-1399
https://www.sandiego.gov/public-library/locations/linda-vista-li

Tuesday, February 25, 2020 5:47:52 PM
19455

Item: 31336092577569
Title: Soap crafting : step-by-step techniques for making 31 unique cold-process soaps
Call no.: 668.12/FAIOLA
Due: 03/17/2020

Item: 31336089913660
Title: The natural soap chef : making luxurious delights from cucumber melon and almond cookie to chai tea and espresso forte
Call no.: 668.12/BARTO
Due: 03/17/2020

Total items: 2

Renew at www.sandiegolibrary.org or by calling your local branch library. Your library card number is needed to renew borrowed items.

5. When both the oil and the lye mixtures are at 110°F, pour the lye mixture into the plastic container with the oils. Blend with your stick blender until the mixture reaches a light trace stage. Stir in the rosemary, then blend a little more until you reach medium trace (see page 26).

6. Pour into a chilled mold and refrigerate, uncovered, for 30 minutes. Remove from the refrigerator; spray the top with isopropyl alcohol, cover loosely with plastic wrap, and refrigerate overnight.

7. Remove from the refrigerator and let sit at room temperature.

8. Unmold 24 hours after pouring into the mold. Cut into bars, spritz with isopropyl alcohol, and place in your curing area.

ROSEMARY-INFUSED OLIVE OIL: Place 2 cups olive oil in a small slow cooker along with several rosemary sprigs. Cover and let simmer on low heat for 4 hours. Let cool, then refrigerate, covered, overnight. Strain before using.

If you don't have a small slow cooker, warm the olive oil and rosemary in a covered heat-safe container set in a saucepan of hot tap water. Either heat on the stove top on warm for several hours, or simply keep refreshing the hot water as it cools. (This method will take longer.)

BASIC 4-OIL SOAP BAR

mix temp
110°F

This recipe is the basis for most of the soaps in this book. You can make it as is—unscented and uncolored—or use it as a jumping-off point for creating your own recipes, adding your choice of colors, fragrances, and exfoliants. To add fragrance, use an online fragrance calculator, select the fragrance you are using, and calculate for cold process soap at 20 ounces.

FRAGRANCE-FREE

OILS

170 grams shea butter

170 grams palm oil

113 grams coconut oil

113 grams olive oil

LYE MIXTURE

78 grams sodium hydroxide (NaOH)

215 grams distilled water

1. Measure the oils into your plastic container. Place the container in a larger pot and pour in enough hot tap water that the container begins to float. Set the pot on the stove and turn the heat to warm. Insert a thermometer into the oil.

2. Goggles and gloves on!

3. Measure the distilled water into a heat-safe glass container. Measure the lye crystals into a separate small glass container. Slowly add the lye crystals to the water, stirring with your spatula as you do so. Do not inhale above this container—beware the fumes! This mixture will heat up quickly. Insert a thermometer into the mixture.

4. Monitor the temperatures of the two containers. You want both to reach 110°F. As needed, refresh the hot water bath or turn the stove burner higher to raise the temperature, or use a cold water or ice bath to bring the temperature down.

5. When both the oils and the lye mixture are at 110°F, pour the lye mixture into the plastic container with the oils. Blend with your stick blender until the mixture reaches medium trace (see page 26).

6. Pour into a chilled mold and refrigerate, uncovered, for 30 minutes. Remove from the refrigerator; spray the top with isopropyl alcohol, cover loosely with plastic wrap, and refrigerate overnight.

7. Remove from the refrigerator and let sit at room temperature.

8. Unmold 24 hours after pouring into the mold. Cut into bars, spritz with isopropyl alcohol, and place in your curing area.

ALMOND COOKIE SOAP

mix temp 110°F *This was one of the first scented bars I ever made, and it's still a favorite. The scent is just delicious! The bar cures to a nice medium-brown color, with speckling from the oatmeal. The finely ground oatmeal acts as an exfoliant.*

OILS

170 grams shea butter

170 grams palm oil

113 grams coconut oil

113 grams olive oil

LYE MIXTURE

78 grams sodium hydroxide (NaOH)

215 grams distilled water

ADD AT TRACE

30 grams almond biscotti fragrance oil

1 tablespoon finely ground rolled oats

1. Measure your fragrance into a small glass container and set out of the way. Measure the oats and set aside.

   Measure the oils into your plastic container. Place the container in a larger pot and pour in enough hot tap water that the container begins to float. Set the pot on the stove and turn the heat to warm. Insert a thermometer into the oil.

2. Goggles and gloves on!

3. Measure the distilled water into a heat-safe glass container. Measure the lye crystals into a separate small glass container. Slowly add the lye crystals to the water, stirring with your spatula as you do so. Do not inhale above this container—there will be fumes that will take your breath away! This mixture will heat up quickly. Insert a thermometer into the mixture.

4. Monitor the temperatures of the two containers. You want both to reach 110°F. As needed, refresh the hot water bath or turn the stove burner higher to raise the temperature, or use a cold water or ice bath to bring temperatures down.

5. When both the oils and the lye mixture are at 110°F, pour the lye mixture into the plastic container with the oils. Blend with your stick blender until the mixture reaches a light trace stage. Add your fragrance and the finely ground oats, then blend until the mixture reaches medium trace (see page 26).

6. Pour into a chilled mold and refrigerate, uncovered, for 30 minutes. Remove from the refrigerator; spray the top with isopropyl alcohol, cover loosely with plastic wrap, and refrigerate overnight.

7. Remove from the refrigerator and let sit at room temperature.

8. Unmold 24 hours after pouring into the mold. Cut into bars, spritz with isopropyl alcohol, and place in your curing area.

CHOCOLATE SOUFFLÉ SOAP

mix temp **100°F**

This bar is decadent! It is an excellent body bar, and with the added clay for "slip," shaving with it is bliss! You'll find yourself lathering up repeatedly just because it smells so good! This bar comes out a deep chocolate color, and the lather has a somewhat tan tint. I've also made this soap in a silicone loaf pan and had it resemble a tray of fudge! Yum!

OILS

227 grams olive oil

170 grams coconut oil

125 grams palm oil

45 grams castor oil

LYE MIXTURE

79 grams sodium hydroxide (NaOH)

215 grams distilled water

ADD AT TRACE

34 grams rich dark chocolate fragrance oil

1½ teaspoons bentonite clay

1. Measure your fragrance and the clay into separate small glass containers and set out of the way.

   Measure the oils into a plastic container. Place the container in a larger pot and pour in enough hot tap water that the container begins to float. Set the pot on the stove and turn the heat to warm. Insert a thermometer into the oil.

2. Goggles and gloves on!

3. Measure the distilled water into a heat-safe glass container. Measure the lye crystals into a separate small glass container. Slowly add the lye crystals to the water, stirring with your spatula as you do so. Do not inhale above this container—there will be fumes that can take your breath away. This mixture will heat up quickly. Insert a thermometer into the mixture.

4. Monitor the temperatures of the two containers. You want both to reach 100°F. This low temperature is necessary for this recipe because it contains castor oil. Castor oil heats up more than other oils during the soap-making process, so mixing at this lower temperature keeps your mixture from getting too hot. As needed, refresh the hot water bath or turn the stove burner higher to raise the temperature, or use a cold water or ice bath to bring the temperature down.

5. When both the oils and the lye mixture are at 100°F, pour the lye mixture into the plastic container with the oils. Blend with your stick blender until the mixture reaches a light trace stage. Pour a little of the mixture into the bentonite clay, mix well to break up any clumps, and add back into the soap mixture. Add your fragrance and blend until the mixture reaches medium trace (see page 26).

6. Pour into your chilled mold and refrigerate, uncovered, for 30 minutes. Remove from the refrigerator; spray the top with isopropyl alcohol, cover loosely with plastic wrap, and refrigerate overnight.

7. Remove from refrigerator and let sit at room temperature.

8. Unmold 48 hours after pouring, cut into bars, and place in your curing area. These bars will be very soft until they cure completely, so handle gently. Let them cure for at least 4 weeks.

LES DUERR LILAC SOAP

mix temp
120°F

I make soap, but my day job is in a library. We have a beautiful garden outside—people stop by just to see our flowers. The gardener places cuttings in a vase at our front desk, and when the lilacs are in bloom, the library smells wonderful! My coworker Bethany lost her mother to lung cancer, and the scent of lilacs always makes her think of her mom. When she heard I was making soap, she asked if I could make a lilac-scented batch for her. This soap is named for Bethany's mom, Leslie Duerr.

OILS

170 grams shea butter

170 grams palm oil

113 grams coconut oil

113 grams alkanet-infused olive oil for purple color (see directions below), or plain olive oil if you want a creamy white bar

LYE MIXTURE

78 grams sodium hydroxide (NaOH)

215 grams distilled water

ADD AT TRACE

25 grams lilac fragrance oil

This soap is mixed at a higher-than-usual temperature and poured into a mold that hasn't been chilled. You want the soap to gel. This will give a nice, even purple coloring to your bars. Make the oil infusion at least a day ahead.

1. Measure your fragrance into a small glass container and set aside.

   Measure the oils into a plastic container. Place the container in a larger pot and pour in enough hot tap water that the container begins to float. Set the pot on the stove and turn the heat to warm. Insert a thermometer into the oil.

2. Goggles and gloves on!

3. Measure the distilled water into a heat-safe glass container. Measure the lye crystals into a separate small glass container. Slowly add the lye crystals to the water, stirring with your spatula as you do so. Do not inhale above this container! This mixture will heat up quickly. Insert a thermometer into the mixture.

4. Monitor the temperatures of the two containers. You want both to reach 120°F. As needed, refresh the hot water bath or turn the stove burner higher to raise the temperature, or use a cold water or ice bath to bring the temperature down.

5. When both the oils and the lye mixture are at 120°F, pour the lye mixture into the plastic container with the oils. Blend with your stick blender until the mixture reaches a light trace stage. (Your mixture will turn from a deep violet to a light violet blue as you mix.) Add your fragrance and blend until the mixture reaches medium trace (see page 26).

6. Pour into your room-temperature mold and cover loosely with plastic wrap. Place the mold in a cardboard box and cover with a lid. Check every half hour and you'll see the soap turning a deep purple, starting from the center and radiating outward. This is the gel stage. When you see this deep color all the way to the edges, you can take the mold out of the box—it doesn't need the insulation anymore and should be allowed to cool down to room temperature. Spray the top with isopropyl alcohol and loosely re-cover with the plastic wrap.

7. Unmold 24 hours after pouring into your mold, cut into bars, spritz with isopropyl alcohol, and place in your curing area.

ALKANET-INFUSED OLIVE OIL: Alkanet root powder can be purchased from soap supply stores and places that sell herbs and spices. Mix 1 teaspoon powdered alkanet root into 130 grams olive oil. Let sit in a covered glass container for at least 24 hours, gently shaking the mixture every so often. Let the alkanet settle to the bottom for several hours. You should be able to measure out 113 grams for the soap recipe without disturbing the sediment at the bottom. That way you get the purple color but don't have to worry about filtering.

MISS B'S LEMON VERBENA SOAP

mix temp
110°F

As a child of the '70s, I was an avid watcher of the television show Little House on the Prairie. *The teacher in the tiny one-room schoolhouse was Miss Beadle. Miss Beadle was pretty and nice, and she wore lemon verbena perfume. She would love this soap!*

FRAGRANCE-FREE

OILS

170 grams shea butter

170 grams palm oil

113 grams coconut oil

113 grams olive oil

LYE MIXTURE

78 grams sodium hydroxide (NaOH)

215 grams distilled water

ADD AT TRACE

30 grams lemon verbena Yankee-type fragrance oil

1 teaspoon dried lemon peel (available in the spice section at the grocery store)

1. Measure your fragrance into a small glass container. Stir in the dried lemon peel and set aside.

   Measure the oils into a plastic container. Place the container in a larger pot and pour in enough hot tap water that the container begins to float. Set the pot on the stove and turn the heat to warm. Insert a thermometer into the oil.

2. Goggles and gloves on!

3. Measure the distilled water into a heat-safe glass container. Measure the lye crystals into a separate small glass container. Slowly add the lye crystals to the water, stirring with your spatula as you do so. Do not inhale above the container! This mixture will heat up quickly. Insert a thermometer into the mixture.

4. Monitor the temperatures of the two containers. You want both to reach 110°F. As needed, refresh the hot water bath or turn the stove burner higher to raise the temperature, or use a cold water or ice bath to bring the temperature down.

5. When both the oils and the lye mixture are at 110°F, pour the lye mixture into the plastic container with the oils. Blend with the stick blender until the mixture reaches a light trace stage. Add the fragrance–lemon peel mix. Blend until the mixture reaches medium trace (see page 26).

6. Pour into a chilled mold and refrigerate, uncovered, for 30 minutes. Remove from the refrigerator; spray the top with isopropyl alcohol, cover loosely with plastic wrap, and refrigerate overnight.

7. Remove from the refrigerator and let sit at room temperature.

8. Unmold 24 hours after pouring into the mold. Cut into bars, spritz with isopropyl alcohol, and place in your curing area.

PINK GRAPEFRUIT SOAP

mix temp *This bar has a great scent to*
115°F *wake you up! Paprika gives
the soap a pinkish orange
color, but it's up to you whether you
want to go through the extra step of
making the paprika-infused oil ahead
of time. Without the paprika, the bar
will be white. Just use regular olive
oil if you decide to leave the bar
uncolored—it will still smell awesome.*

OILS

170 grams shea butter

170 grams palm oil

113 grams coconut oil

113 grams paprika-
infused olive oil (see
directions below)

LYE MIXTURE

78 grams sodium
hydroxide (NaOH)

215 grams distilled water

ADD AT TRACE

34 grams pink grapefruit
fragrance oil

1. Measure your fragrance into a small glass container and set aside.

   Measure the oils into a plastic container. Place the container in a larger
   pot and pour in enough hot tap water that the container begins to float.
   Set the pot on the stove and turn the heat to warm. Insert a thermometer
   into the oil.

2. Goggles and gloves on!

3. Measure the distilled water into a heat-safe glass container. Measure
   the lye crystals into a separate small glass container. Slowly add the
   lye crystals to the water, stirring with your spatula as you do so. Do
   not inhale above this container—there will be fumes that can take your
   breath away. This mixture will heat up quickly. Insert a thermometer into
   the lye mixture.

4. Monitor the temperatures of the two containers. You want both to reach 115°F. As needed, refresh the hot water bath or turn the stove burner higher to raise the temperature, or use a cold water or ice bath to bring the temperature down.

5. When both the oils and the lye mixture are at 115°F, pour the lye mixture into the plastic container with the oils. Blend with your stick blender until the mixture reaches a light trace stage. Add your fragrance. Blend until the mixture reaches medium trace (see page 26).

6. Pour into your chilled mold. For the top shown in the photograph, tear off small pieces of fresh grapefruit peel, trim away any excess pith (white part), and lightly place shiny side down to cover the loaf top. Lightly cover with plastic and refrigerate overnight.

7. Remove from the refrigerator and let sit at room temperature.

8. Unmold 24 hours after pouring into your mold, cut into bars, spritz with isopropyl alcohol, and place in your curing area.

PAPRIKA-INFUSED OLIVE OIL: In a heat-safe glass container, combine 2 teaspoons of paprika with 125 grams of olive oil. Set this container in a larger container, pour in just enough hot tap water that the inner container starts to float, and cover. Leave overnight, then strain through a coffee filter. The oil will be a bright orange, but the end result in your bar of soap will be a pinkish orange.

SAGE & LEMONGRASS SOAP

mix temp 110°F *This soap has a crisp, fresh scent. Anyone who loves being outdoors will love it. The bar has a light, translucent sage color, with darker flecks. It really is a beautiful soap.*

OILS

170 grams shea butter

170 grams palm oil

113 grams coconut oil

113 grams sage-infused olive oil (see directions below)

LYE MIXTURE

78 grams sodium hydroxide (NaOH)

215 grams distilled water

ADD AT TRACE

25 grams sage and lemongrass fragrance oil

½ teaspoon sage paste, for color (see directions below)

1. Measure your fragrance into a small glass container. Stir in the sage paste and set aside.

   Measure the oils into a plastic container. Place in a larger pot and pour in enough hot tap water that the container begins to float. Set the pot on the stove and turn the heat to warm. Insert a thermometer into the oil.

2. Goggles and gloves on!

3. Measure the distilled water into a heat-safe glass container. Measure the lye crystals into a separate small glass container. Slowly add the lye crystals to the water, stirring with your spatula as you do so. Do not inhale above this container—be cautious of any fumes. This mixture will heat up quickly. Insert a thermometer into the mixture.

4. Monitor the temperatures of the two containers. You want both to reach 110°F. As needed, refresh the hot water bath or turn the stove burner higher to raise the temperature, or use a cold water or ice bath to bring the temperature down.

5. When both the oils and the lye mixture are at 110°F, pour the lye mixture into the plastic container with the oils. Blend with your stick blender until the mixture reaches a light trace stage. Add the fragrance-sage mixture. Blend until the mixture reaches medium trace (see page 26).

6. Pour into a chilled mold and refrigerate, uncovered, for 30 minutes. Remove from the refrigerator; spray the top with isopropyl alcohol, cover loosely with plastic wrap, and refrigerate overnight.

7. Remove from the refrigerator and let sit at room temperature.

8. Unmold 24 hours after pouring into the mold. Cut into bars, spritz with isopropyl alcohol, and place in your curing area.

SAGE-INFUSED OLIVE OIL: Add 2 teaspoons sage to 125 grams olive oil, place the container in a hot tap water bath, cover, and let steep for several hours. Replenish the hot water as needed. Strain through a coffee filter.

SAGE PASTE: Finely chop some dried sage and mix with a little olive oil to make a paste. Push through a fine mesh strainer. Use a knife to scrape off what comes through the strainer until you have ½ teaspoon.

SHAVING SOAP

mix temp **100°F** *I make this recipe using a 2-foot piece of 2-inch PVC pipe with two ends caps as a mold and a 2-foot piece of 1½-inch PVC pipe with one end cap for unmolding. This makes a bar that's perfect for using in a shaving mug with a shaving brush. You can also make it in a regular loaf mold. The soap used has a nice, masculine scent. If you're someone like me who puts on your husband or boyfriend's shirt just to smell his cologne, you will probably love this fragrance.*

MAKES 16 OUNCES (ABOUT 10 BARS)

OILS

181 grams olive oil

136 grams coconut oil

100 grams palm oil

36 grams castor oil

LYE MIXTURE

64 grams sodium hydroxide (NaOH)

172 grams distilled water

ADD AT TRACE

17 grams spiced mahogany fragrance oil

2 teaspoons bentonite clay

1. Measure your fragrance and clay into separate small glass containers and set aside.

   Measure the oils into a plastic container. Place the container in a larger pot and pour in enough hot tap water that the container begins to float. Set the pot on the stove and turn the heat to warm. Insert a thermometer into the oil.

2. Goggles and gloves on!

3. Measure the distilled water into a heat-safe glass container. Measure the lye crystals into a separate small glass container. Slowly add the lye crystals to the water, stirring with your spatula as you do so. Do not inhale above this container—remember, there will be fumes. This mixture will heat up quickly. Insert a thermometer into the mixture.

4. Monitor the temperatures of the two containers. You want both to reach 100°F. This lower-than-usual temperature is necessary because castor

oil heats up more than other oils in the soap-making process. As needed, refresh the hot water bath or turn the stove burner higher to raise the temperature, or use a cold water or ice bath to bring the temperature down.

5. When both the oils and the lye mixture are at 100°F, pour the lye mixture into the plastic container with the oils. Blend with your stick blender until the mixture reaches a light trace stage (see page 26). Pour a little of the mixture into the bentonite clay, mix well to break up any clumps, and add back in. Blend in your fragrance.

6. Cap the end of a 2-foot section of 2-inch PVC pipe and tape closed. Pour in the soap mixture at light trace. Tap the pipe a few times to release any air bubbles. Cap the other end and let sit for 24 to 48 hours at room temperature.

7. To unmold, I put the pipe in the freezer for about an hour, then take it out and drop it on the ground a few times to loosen the soap. I use a 2-foot section of 1½-inch PVC pipe with an end cap to push out the soap. Your tube of soap will probably have some frost on it—just set it aside and let it warm up, then cut into little round bars and place in your curing area.

When the bars fully cure, I use a vegetable peeler to bevel the top and bottom edges. It really makes them look finished.

STANK DOG SOAP
(FOR CANINES AND THEIR COMPANIONS)

mix temp
90°F

This bar will deodorize anyone, canine or human! The idea for the soap came from my Vizsla dog, Penelope. Vizslas are known as Velcro dogs—they like to stick with their humans all the time. Penelope has been known to hop in while a family member is showering. Having a soap that serves double duty—what a brilliant idea!

FRAGRANCE-FREE

OILS

170 grams castor oil

170 grams palm oil

142 grams coconut oil

85 grams olive oil

LYE MIXTURE

79 grams sodium hydroxide (NaOH)

215 grams distilled water

ADD AT TRACE

17 grams lemongrass essential oil

4 grams peppermint essential oil

4 grams tea tree essential oil

1. Measure your essential oils into a small glass container and set aside.

   Measure the oils into a plastic container. Place the container in a larger pot and pour in enough hot tap water that the container begins to float. Set the pot on the stove and turn the heat to warm. Insert a thermometer into the oil.

2. Goggles and gloves on!

3. Measure the distilled water into a heat-safe glass container. Measure the lye crystals into a separate small glass container. Slowly add the lye crystals to the water, stirring with your spatula as you do so. Do not inhale above this container—I really can't repeat often enough about

watching out for fumes. This mixture will heat up quickly. Insert a thermometer into the mixture.

4. Monitor the temperatures of the two containers. You want both to reach 90°F. As needed, refresh the hot water bath or turn the stove burner higher to raise the temperature, or use a cold water or ice bath to bring the temperature down.

5. When both the oils and the lye mixture are at 90°F, pour the lye mixture into the plastic container with the oils. Blend with your stick blender until the mixture reaches a light trace stage. Add your fragrances and blend until the mixture reaches medium trace (see page 26).

6. Pour into a chilled mold and refrigerate, uncovered, for 30 minutes. Remove from the refrigerator; spray the top with isopropyl alcohol, cover loosely with plastic wrap, and refrigerate overnight.

7. Remove from the refrigerator and let sit at room temperature.

8. Unmold 24 hours after pouring into the mold. Cut into bars, spritz with isopropyl alcohol, and place in your curing area.

CHAPTER 4
COFFEE, TEA, & STOUT RECIPES

The following recipes make excellent soaps, but require a little extra prep work:

Coffee soaps are the perfect pick-me-up in bar form! Make a very strong coffee with distilled water. You can either use your coffee maker or just add loose grounds to boiling water and let them steep. (Be sure to filter the coffee if you use the steeping method.) Chill your coffee mixture before mixing it with lye. Coffee grounds also act as a great exfoliant in soap, and coffee beans can be used to decorate the tops of the bars.

Tea can be used to add color to soap, and the leaves exfoliate. Use distilled water to make the tea, from either tea bags or loose tea. A tea bag eliminates having to strain later, but I find that the loose leaves produce stronger tea. I chill my tea after it has steeped to a dark-enough color. Chilled tea will help you get to your mixing temperature sooner.

Beer or stout in soap results in a bar that has wonderful lather. Boil to remove the alcohol, let cool, and then chill until it's flat. You don't want any carbonation left or your lye mixture will volcano over. That is not something you want to happen. Adding lye to beer or stout produces an awful smell, but don't worry—the odor won't be in your bar of soap.

ESPRESSO FORTE SOAP

mix temp
110°F

This recipe can be made with or without the coffee fragrance. Without it, the bars will be a medium brown color and have just a faint coffee scent. With fragrance, the bars will be a deep brown and have a nice chocolate-espresso aroma. You can also place roasted espresso beans on top (not too many). This adds to the great coffee scent. The beans will come off with use, but it's before you use the bar that you want it to look great!

OILS

170 grams shea butter

170 grams palm oil

113 grams coconut oil

113 grams olive oil

LYE MIXTURE

78 grams sodium hydroxide (NaOH)

215 grams chilled strong espresso (made with distilled water)

ADD AT TRACE

½ teaspoon coffee grounds (from making your strong espresso)

34 grams chocolate-espresso fragrance oil (optional)

1. Measure your fragrance, if using, into a small glass container. Add the coffee grounds and set aside.

   Measure the oils into a plastic container. Place the container in a larger pot and pour in enough hot tap water that the container begins to float. Set the pot on the stove and turn the heat to warm. Insert a thermometer into the oils.

2. Goggles and gloves on!

3. Measure your chilled espresso into a heat-safe glass container. Measure the lye crystals into a separate small glass container. Slowly add the lye crystals to the coffee, stirring with your spatula as you do so. Do not inhale above this container—the fumes will be especially strong. This mixture will heat up quickly. Insert a thermometer into the mixture.

4. Monitor the temperatures of the two containers. You want both to reach 110°F. As needed, refresh the hot water bath or turn the stove burner higher to raise the temperature, or use a cold water or ice bath to bring the temperature down.

5. When both the oils and the lye mixture are at 110°F, pour the lye mixture into the plastic container with the oils. Blend with your stick blender until the mixture reaches a light trace stage. Add the fragrance–coffee grounds mixture and blend until the mixture reaches medium trace (see page 26).

6. Pour into a chilled mold and arrange 12 to 16 espresso beans on top for decoration, if desired. Spray the top with isopropyl alcohol, cover loosely with plastic wrap, and refrigerate overnight.

7. Remove from the refrigerator and let sit at room temperature.

8. Unmold 24 hours after pouring into the mold. Cut into bars, spritz with isopropyl alcohol, and place in your curing area.

CHAI TEA SOAP

mix temp **110°F** *Chai tea is a milky spiced beverage from India. Although this version is milk-free, it still has the same comforting, spicy fragrance. The bar turns medium to dark brown, producing white lather. The tea leaves are great exfoliants, and the honey helps to moisturize.*

OILS

170 grams shea butter

170 grams palm oil

113 grams coconut oil

113 grams olive oil

LYE MIXTURE

78 grams sodium hydroxide (NaOH)

215 grams chilled chai tea (see directions below)

ADD AT TRACE

30 grams chai tea fragrance oil

1 teaspoon chai tea leaves (from making your chai tea)

1 tablespoon honey

1. Measure your fragrance into a small glass container. Add the 1 teaspoon tea leaves and set aside.

   Measure the oils into a plastic container. Place the container in a larger pot and pour in enough hot tap water that the container begins to float. Set the pot on the stove and turn the heat to warm. Insert a thermometer into the oils.

2. Goggles and gloves on!

3. Measure the chilled tea into a heat-safe glass container. Measure the lye crystals into a separate small glass container. Slowly add the lye crystals to the tea, stirring with your spatula as you do so. Do not inhale above this container—the fumes will be very strong. This mixture will heat up quickly. Insert a thermometer into the mixture.

4. Monitor the temperatures of the two containers. You want both to reach 110°F. As needed, refresh the hot water bath or turn the stove burner higher to raise the temperature, or use a cold water or ice bath to bring the temperature down.

5. When both the oils and the lye mixture are at 110°F, pour the lye mixture into the plastic container with the oils. Blend with your stick blender until the mixture reaches a light trace stage. Add your fragrance–tea leaves mixture and the honey. Honey accelerates trace, so be prepared to move quickly! Blend until the mixture reaches medium trace (see page 26).

6. Pour into a chilled mold and refrigerate, uncovered, for 30 minutes. Remove from the refrigerator; spray the top with isopropyl alcohol, cover loosely with plastic wrap, and refrigerate overnight.

7. Remove from refrigerator and let sit at room temperature.

8. Unmold 24 hours after pouring into the mold. Cut into bars, spritz with isopropyl alcohol, and place in your curing area.

CHAI TEA: Add the leaves from 2 chai tea bags to 250 grams boiling distilled water; let steep until the color is very dark. Chill. Strain with a fine strainer and set the tea leaves aside.

BLACK TEA SOAP

mix temp
110°F

Smoky and sophisticated, this soap smells of roasted tea leaves and tobacco, with just a hint of musk. You don't have to love tobacco to love this soap. Its fragrance is bold and unusual, the type of scent that grows on you. Besides, the soap is beautiful to look at! There's a streakiness to the bar that more mixing might eliminate, but I love it this way.

OILS

170 grams shea butter

170 grams palm oil

113 grams coconut oil

113 grams olive oil

LYE MIXTURE

78 grams sodium hydroxide (NaOH)

215 grams chilled strong black tea (see directions below)

ADD AT TRACE

34 grams black tea fragrance oil

¼ teaspoon black tea leaves (from making your tea)

1. Measure your fragrance into a small glass container. Add the ¼ teaspoon tea leaves and set aside.

   Measure the oils into a plastic container. Place the container in a larger pot and pour in enough hot tap water that the container begins to float. Set the pot on the stove and turn the heat to warm. Insert a thermometer into the oils.

2. Goggles and gloves on!

3. Measure the chilled tea into a heat-safe glass container. Measure the lye crystals into a separate small glass container. Slowly add the lye crystals to the tea, stirring with your spatula as you do so. Do not inhale above this container—the fumes will be very strong. This mixture will heat up quickly. Insert a thermometer into the mixture.

4. Monitor the temperatures of the two containers. You want both to reach 110°F. As needed, refresh the hot water bath or turn the stove burner

higher to raise the temperature, or use a cold water or ice bath to bring the temperature down.

5. When both the oils and the lye mixture are at 110°F, pour the lye mixture into the plastic container with the oils. Blend with your stick blender until the mixture reaches a light trace stage, then add the fragrance–tea leaves mixture. Blend until the mixture reaches medium trace (see page 26).

6. Pour into a chilled mold and refrigerate, uncovered, for 30 minutes. Remove from the refrigerator; spray the top with isopropyl alcohol, cover loosely with plastic wrap, and refrigerate overnight.

7. Remove from refrigerator and let sit at room temperature.

8. Unmold 24 hours after pouring into the mold. Cut into bars, spritz with isopropyl alcohol, and place in your curing area.

BLACK TEA: Add the leaves from 2 bags of black tea to 250 grams boiling distilled water; let steep until the color is very dark. Chill. Strain with a fine strainer and set the tea leaves aside.

PEPPERMINT TEA SOAP

mix temp **110°F** *What can I say about peppermint soap? People love, love, love peppermint soap! The fragrance helps to wake you up and get you moving in the morning. Peppermint essential oil also has a cooling effect on your skin. Many people swear by my peppermint soap to soothe aching joints. I don't make any health claims—I'm just happy they like my soap!*

OILS

170 grams shea butter

170 grams palm oil

113 grams coconut oil

113 grams olive oil

LYE MIXTURE

78 grams sodium hydroxide (NaOH)

215 grams chilled strong peppermint tea (see directions below)

ADD AT TRACE

9 grams peppermint essential oil, 2nd distill

½ teaspoon peppermint tea leaves (from making your tea)

1. Measure your fragrance into a small glass container. Add the ½ teaspoon tea leaves and set aside.

   Measure the oils into a plastic container. Place the container in a larger pot and pour in enough hot tap water that the container begins to float. Set the pot on the stove and turn the heat to warm. Insert a thermometer into the oils.

2. Goggles and gloves on!

3. Measure the chilled tea into a heat-safe glass container. Measure the lye crystals into a separate small glass container. Slowly add the lye crystals to the tea, stirring with your spatula as you do so. Do not inhale above this container—the fumes will be very strong. This mixture will heat up quickly. Insert a thermometer into the mixture.

4. Monitor the temperatures of the two containers. You want both to reach 110°F. As needed, refresh the hot water bath or turn the stove burner higher to raise the temperature, or use a cold water or ice bath to bring the temperature down.

5. When both the oils and the lye mixture are at 110°F, pour the lye mixture into the plastic container with the oils. Blend with your stick blender until the mixture reaches a light trace stage, then add your fragrance–tea leaves mixture. Blend until the mixture reaches medium trace (see page 26).

6. Pour into a chilled mold and refrigerate, uncovered, for 30 minutes. Remove from the refrigerator; spray the top with isopropyl alcohol, cover loosely with plastic wrap, and refrigerate overnight.

7. Remove from refrigerator and let sit at room temperature.

8. Unmold 24 hours after pouring into the mold. Cut into bars, spritz with isopropyl alcohol, and place in your curing area.

PEPPERMINT TEA: Add tea leaves from 2 peppermint tea bags to 250 grams boiling distilled water; let steep until the color is very dark. Chill. Strain with a fine strainer and set the tea leaves aside.

BABY ROSE SOAP

mix temp
110°F

This soap reminds me a bit of baby powder, with a pleasant rose scent that isn't cloying or overpowering. Raspberry tea adds color and texture. If you use plain distilled water instead of the tea, the bars will be a creamy white color.

OILS

170 grams shea butter

170 grams palm oil

113 grams coconut oil

113 grams olive oil

LYE MIXTURE

78 grams sodium hydroxide (NaOH)

215 grams chilled red raspberry herbal tea (see directions below)

ADD AT TRACE

25 grams baby rose fragrance oil

½ teaspoon red raspberry tea leaves (from making your tea)

1. Measure your fragrance into a small glass container. Add the ½ teaspoon tea leaves and set aside.

   Measure the oils into a plastic container. Place the container in a larger pot and pour in enough hot tap water that the container begins to float. Set the pot on the stove and turn the heat to warm. Insert a thermometer into the oils.

2. Goggles and gloves on!

3. Measure the chilled tea into a heat-safe glass container. Measure the lye crystals into a separate small glass container. Slowly add the lye crystals to the tea, stirring with your spatula as you do so. Do not inhale above this container—the fumes will be very strong. This mixture will heat up quickly. Insert a thermometer into the mixture.

4. Monitor the temperatures of the two containers. You want both to reach 110°F. As needed, refresh the hot water bath or turn the stove burner higher to raise the temperature, or use a cold water or ice bath to bring the temperature down.

5. When both the oils and the lye mixture are at 110°F, pour the lye mixture into the plastic container with the oils. Blend with your stick blender until the mixture reaches a light trace stage, then add your fragrance–tea leaves mixture. Blend until the mixture reaches medium trace (see page 26).

6. Pour into a chilled mold and refrigerate, uncovered, for 30 minutes. Remove from the refrigerator; spray the top with isopropyl alcohol, cover loosely with plastic wrap, and refrigerate overnight.

7. Remove from refrigerator and let sit at room temperature.

8. Unmold 24 hours after pouring into the mold. Cut into bars, spritz with isopropyl alcohol, and place in your curing area.

RED RASPBERRY HERBAL TEA: Add the leaves from 2 red raspberry herbal tea bags to 250 grams boiling distilled water; let steep until the color is very dark. Chill. Strain with a fine strainer and set the tea leaves aside.

HIPPIE SOAP

mix temp
105°F

This soap is the result of the question, "What's the proper way to pronounce nag champa?" I had purchased some of this fragrance to try in a recipe, and every time I told someone what the fragrance was, I'd hesitate over the pronunciation. My coworker came up with the solution of calling it Hippie Soap. Well, I couldn't do that without adding hemp oil—this book's only recipe containing hemp oil.

OILS

153 grams shea butter

170 grams palm oil

113 grams coconut oil

108 grams olive oil

23 grams hemp oil

LYE MIXTURE

78 grams sodium hydroxide (NaOH)

215 grams chilled Indian spice tea or chai tea (see directions below)

ADD AT TRACE

30 grams nag champa fragrance oil

1 teaspoon Indian spice or chai tea leaves (from making your tea)

I tablespoon honey

1. Measure your fragrance into a small glass container. Add the 1 teaspoon tea leaves and set aside.

   Measure the oils into a plastic container. Place the container in a larger pot and pour in enough hot tap water that the container begins to float. Set the pot on the stove and turn the heat to warm. Insert a thermometer into the oils.

2. Goggles and gloves on!

3. Measure the chilled tea into a heat-safe glass container. Measure the lye crystals into a separate small glass container. Slowly add the lye crystals to the tea, stirring with your spatula as you do so. Do not inhale above this container—the fumes will be very strong. This mixture will heat up quickly. Insert a thermometer into the mixture.

4. Monitor the temperatures of the two containers. You want both to reach 105°F. As needed, refresh the hot water bath or turn the stove burner higher to raise the temperature, or use a cold water or ice bath to bring the temperature down.

5. When both the oils and the lye mixture are at 105°F, pour the lye mixture into the plastic container with the oils. Blend with your stick blender until the mixture reaches a light trace stage, then add your fragrance–tea leaves mixture and the honey. Honey accelerates trace, so be prepared to move quickly! Blend until the mixture reaches medium trace (see page 26).

6. Pour into a chilled mold and refrigerate, uncovered, for 30 minutes. Remove from the refrigerator; spray the top with isopropyl alcohol, cover loosely with plastic wrap, and refrigerate overnight.

7. Remove from refrigerator and let sit at room temperature.

8. Unmold 24 hours after pouring into the mold. Cut into bars, spritz with isopropyl alcohol, and place in your curing area.

INDIAN SPICE TEA OR CHAI TEA: Add the leaves from 2 Indian spice or chai tea bags to 250 grams boiling distilled water; let steep until very dark. Chill. Strain with a fine strainer and set the tea leaves aside.

GUINNESS® STOUT SOAP

┃ mix temp
105°F

Beer in soap! This one isn't just for the guys. My daughter thinks that Guinness smells like black olives. "What do you know?" I said. "You're 14!" Paige was right, though—the smell of the finished soap is a bit like black olives and yeast. It's a very clean scent, and the lather is fabulous!

FRAGRANCE-FREE

OILS

170 grams shea butter

170 grams palm oil

113 grams coconut oil

113 grams olive oil

LYE MIXTURE

78 grams sodium hydroxide (NaOH)

215 grams Guinness stout (boil 5 minutes to remove the alcohol, then chill to let it go flat)

1. Measure the oils into a plastic container. Place the container in a larger pot and pour in enough hot tap water that the container begins to float. Set the pot on the stove and turn the heat to warm. Insert a thermometer into the oils.

2. Goggles and gloves on!

3. Measure the chilled Guinness into a heat-safe glass container. Measure the lye crystals into a separate small glass container. Slowly add the lye crystals to the Guinness, stirring with your spatula as you do so. The lye-Guinness mixture will reek! Be sure to have adequate ventilation. This mixture will heat up quickly. Insert a thermometer into the mixture.

4. Monitor the temperatures of the two containers. You want both to reach 105°F. As needed, refresh the hot water bath or turn the stove higher to raise the temperature, or use a cold water or ice bath to bring the temperature down.

5. When both the oils and the lye mixture are at 105°F, pour the lye mixture into the plastic container with the oils. Blend with your stick blender until the mixture reaches medium trace (see page 26). Your soap batter will be a deep brown, but the finished soap will lighten to a creamy camel color.

6. Pour into a chilled mold and refrigerate, uncovered, for 30 minutes. Remove from the refrigerator; spray the top with isopropyl alcohol, cover loosely with plastic wrap, and refrigerate overnight.

7. Remove from refrigerator and let sit at room temperature.

8. Unmold 24 hours after pouring into the mold. Cut into bars, spritz with isopropyl alcohol, and place in your curing area.

OCEAN RAIN SOAP

mix temp **105°F**

This is the same as Guinness Stout Soap (page 68), but with an added fragrance, ocean rain. This lingering scent is crisp and clean, perfect for men and women. I also use this scent in my Head-to-Toe Shampoo Bar (page 84).

OILS	LYE MIXTURE	ADD AT TRACE
170 grams shea butter	78 grams sodium hydroxide (NaOH)	30 grams ocean rain fragrance oil
170 grams palm oil	215 grams Guinness stout (boil 5 minutes to remove the alcohol, then chill to let it go flat)	
113 grams coconut oil		
113 grams olive oil		

1. Measure your fragrance oil into a small glass container and set aside.

   Measure the oils into a plastic container. Place the container in a larger pot and pour in enough hot tap water that the container begins to float. Set the pot on the stove and turn the heat to warm. Insert a thermometer into the oils.

2. Goggles and gloves on!

3. Measure the chilled Guinness into a heat-safe glass container. Measure the lye crystals into a separate small glass container. Slowly add the lye crystals to the Guinness, stirring with your spatula as you do so. The lye-Guinness mixture will reek! Be sure to have adequate ventilation. This mixture will heat up quickly. Insert a thermometer into the mixture.

4. Monitor the temperatures of the two containers. You want both to reach 105°F. As needed, refresh the hot water bath or turn the stove burner

higher to raise the temperature, or use a cold water or ice bath to bring the temperature down.

5. When both the oils and the lye mixture are at 105°F, pour the lye mixture into the plastic container with the oils. Blend with your stick blender until the mixture reaches a light trace stage, then add your fragrance oil. Blend until the mixture reaches medium trace (see page 26).

6. Pour into a chilled mold and refrigerate, uncovered, for 30 minutes. Remove from the refrigerator; spray the top with isopropyl alcohol, cover loosely with plastic wrap, and refrigerate overnight.

7. Remove from refrigerator and let sit at room temperature.

8. Unmold 24 hours after pouring into the mold. Cut into bars, spritz with isopropyl alcohol, and place in your curing area.

CHAPTER 5

GOAT'S MILK, COCONUT MILK, & PURÉE RECIPES

If you happen to know someone who raises goats, ask if they can provide you with goat milk. Otherwise, you may be able to find it at your grocery store. It's a bit of a drive to the Trader Joe's where I get mine, so I buy several quarts at a time and freeze it in sandwich-size freezer bags. I measure 100 grams into each bag and write the weight and date on the bag. (The milk should always be weighed before it is frozen.) I make sure the bag is sealed, then lay it flat and freeze it. I like to break the frozen milk into pieces before I take it out of the bag. Laying it flat to freeze it makes that easy.

Since lye will heat up your liquid, frozen goat's milk is ideal—it won't scorch or burn as easily as chilled goat's milk. Add the lye crystals to the frozen milk slowly, stirring as the milk melts.

Note that a by-product of making soap with goat's milk is a lovely ammonia odor (said with sarcasm). Don't let this smell fool you—it will fade and leave you with great-smelling soap. I promise.

Coconut milk is available at any grocery store—just be sure the can says "milk" and not "cream." Store the cans in your fridge until you are ready to use them. Chilling the milk will help keep the temperature down and prevent scorching.

Sometimes I'll "flavor" my soaps with purées made from fresh fruits or vegetables. Another easy option is to buy ready-made purée in the form of baby food.

When adding lye to a purée, I always use an ice bath. Find a plastic container big enough that your glass container will fit inside, and pour ice and cool water around the outside of the glass container. This will keep the temperature down and keep your purée from scorching.

GOAT'S MILK, OATMEAL, & HONEY SOAP

mix temp
90°F

This soap smells just like a delicious bowl of oatmeal. Oatmeal exfoliates and helps soothe dry skin, and the addition of honey makes the bar even more moisturizing. Fragrance oils are available in an oatmeal scent, but I like this one au natural!

FRAGRANCE-FREE

OILS
170 grams shea butter

170 grams palm oil

113 grams coconut oil

113 grams olive oil

LYE MIXTURE
78 grams sodium hydroxide (NaOH)

215 grams frozen goat's milk (weighed before freezing)

ADD AT TRACE
1 tablespoon honey

2 tablespoons finely ground rolled oats

1. Measure the oils into a plastic container. Place the container in a larger pot and pour in enough hot tap water that the container begins to float. Set the pot on the stove and turn the heat to warm. Insert a thermometer into the oils. When all the solids oils have melted, it's time to proceed.

2. Goggles and gloves on!

3. Take your goat's milk out of the freezer, break into chunks, and put in a heat-proof glass container; place the container in an ice water bath. Measure the lye crystals into a separate small glass container. Slowly add the lye crystals to the milk, stirring with your spatula as you do so. Insert a thermometer into the mixture.

   The goat's milk will darken in color and start to melt. Keep stirring. If you notice the temperature rising above 140°F, add more ice to the ice bath. Do not inhale above this container!

4. Monitor the temperatures of the two containers. You want both to reach 90°F. As needed, refresh the hot water bath or turn the stove burner higher to raise the temperature, or add ice to the cold water bath to bring the temperature down.

5. When both the oils and the lye mixture are at 90°F, pour the lye mixture into the plastic container with the oils. Blend with your stick blender until the mixture reaches a light trace stage, then add the honey and the finely ground oats. Blend with the stick blender until the mixture reaches medium trace (see page 26).

6. Pour into your chilled mold. For a cool-looking top, sprinkle some rolled oats across the top. Cut a piece of bubble wrap to fit the top of the loaf. Lay the bubble wrap across the loaf and push it gently into the soap, just enough to make an impression. This will give you a top that looks like a honeycomb and will help prevent ash from forming on the bars. Refrigerate overnight.

7. Remove from refrigerator and let sit at room temperature.

8. Remove the bubble wrap 24 hours after pouring into the mold. Unmold, cut into bars, spritz with isopropyl alcohol, and place in your curing area.

JUICED BARS

mix temp **110°F**

With this recipe, I was trying to create a creamsicle soap. I combined a juicy orange scent with all the skin benefits derived from goat's milk. There's also just a bit of orange peel added to exfoliate.

OILS

170 grams shea butter

170 grams palm oil

113 grams coconut oil

113 grams olive oil

LYE MIXTURE

78 grams sodium hydroxide (NaOH)

215 grams frozen goat's milk (weighed before freezing)

ADD AT TRACE

34 grams orange-peel– cybilla fragrance oil

1 teaspoon dried orange peel (available in the spice section of the grocery store)

1. Measure your fragrance into a glass container, add the dried orange peel, and set aside.

   Measure the oils into a plastic container. Place the container in a larger pot and pour in enough hot tap water that the container begins to float. Set the pot on the stove and turn the heat to warm. Insert a thermometer into the oils.

2. Goggles and gloves on!

3. Take the goat's milk out of the freezer, break it into chunks, and put in a heat-safe glass container; place the container in an ice water bath. Measure the lye crystals into a separate small glass container. Slowly add the lye crystals to the milk, stirring with your spatula as you do so. Insert a thermometer into the mixture.

The goat's milk will darken in color and start to melt; keep stirring. If you notice the temperature rising above 140°F, add more ice to the cold water bath. Do not inhale above this container!

4. Monitor the temperatures of the two containers. You want both to reach 110°F. As needed, refresh the hot water bath or turn the stove burner higher to raise the temperature, or add ice to the cold water bath to bring the temperature down.

5. When both the oils and the lye mixture are at 110°F, pour the lye mixture into the plastic container with the oils. Blend with your stick blender until the mixture reaches a light trace stage, then add the fragrance-peel mixture. Blend until the mixture reaches medium trace (see page 26).

6. Pour into a chilled mold and refrigerate, uncovered, for 30 minutes. Remove from the refrigerator; spray the top with isopropyl alcohol, cover loosely with plastic wrap, and refrigerate overnight.

7. Remove from refrigerator and let sit at room temperature.

8. Unmold 24 hours after pouring into the mold. Cut into bars, spritz with isopropyl alcohol, and place in your curing area.

JUST FACE IT!

mix temp **100°F**

This is an awesome facial soap! I've superfatted this recipe more than usual to create a mild bar that won't dry out your skin. Special ingredients contribute to beautiful, healthy skin: honey is a humectant and microbial, goat's milk contains lactic and caprylic acids that help maintain beautiful skin, bentonite clay gives extra "slip" to soap and is absorbent (great for oily skin), and tea tree oil is a natural antiseptic.

OIL

567 grams olive oil

LYE MIXTURE

71 grams sodium hydroxide (NaOH)

215 grams frozen goat's milk (weighed before freezing)

ADD AT TRACE

1 tablespoon honey

8 grams tea tree essential oil

2 teaspoons bentonite clay

1. Measure the tea tree oil and bentonite clay into separate glass containers and set aside.

   Measure the olive oil into a plastic container. Place the container in a larger pot and pour in enough hot tap water that the container begins to float. Set the pot on the stove and turn the heat to warm. Insert a thermometer into the oil.

2. Goggles and gloves on!

3. Take the goat's milk out of the freezer, break into chunks, and put in a heat-safe glass container; place the container in an ice water bath. Measure the lye crystals into a separate small glass container. Slowly add the lye crystals to the milk, stirring with your spatula as you do so. Insert a thermometer into the mixture.

The goat's milk will darken in color and start to melt; keep stirring. If you notice the temperature rising above 140°F, add more ice to the cold water bath. Do not inhale above this container!

4. Monitor the temperatures of the two containers. You want both to reach 100°F. As needed, refresh the hot water bath or turn the stove burner higher to raise the temperature, or add ice to the cold water bath to bring the temperature down.

5. When both the oil and the lye mixture are at 100°F, pour the lye mixture into the plastic container with the oil. Blend with your stick blender until the mixture reaches a light trace stage. Pour a little of the mixture into the bentonite clay, mix well to break up any clumps, and add back into the soap mixture. Add the honey and tea tree oil. Blend until the mixture reaches medium trace (see page 26).

6. Pour into your chilled mold. To decorate with bubble wrap, cut a piece of bubble wrap to fit the top of the loaf. Lay it across the loaf and push it gently into the soap, just enough to make an impression. This will give you a top that looks like a honeycomb and will help prevent ash from forming on the bars. Refrigerate overnight.

7. Remove from refrigerator and let sit at room temperature.

8. Remove the bubble wrap 24 hours after pouring into the mold. Unmold, cut into bars, spritz with isopropyl alcohol, and place in your curing area.

PIÑA COLADA SOAP

mix temp
110°F

When I first started making soap, every bar smelled liked baked goods. My husband, Rick, kept asking me, "When are you going to make some fruity soap. I like fruity soap!" This is Rick's fruity soap.

OILS	LYE MIXTURE	ADD AT TRACE
170 grams shea butter	78 grams sodium hydroxide (NaOH)	25 grams pineapple-cilantro fragrance oil
170 grams palm oil		
113 grams coconut oil	215 grams chilled coconut milk	8 grams coconut-cybilla fragrance oil
113 grams olive oil		

1. Measure your fragrances into a small glass container and set aside.

   Measure the oils into a plastic container. Place the container in a larger pot and pour in enough hot tap water that the container begins to float. Set the pot on the stove and turn the heat to warm. Insert a thermometer into the oils.

2. Goggles and gloves on!

3. Measure the chilled coconut milk into a heat-safe glass container and set the container into an ice water bath. Measure the lye crystals into a separate small glass container. Slowly add the lye crystals to the coconut milk, stirring with your spatula as you do so. Insert a thermometer into the mixture.

   The coconut milk will darken in color and thicken; keep stirring. If you notice the temperature rising above 140°F, add more ice to your cold water bath. Do not inhale above this container!

4. Monitor the temperatures of the two containers. You want both to reach 110°F. As needed, refresh the hot water bath or turn the stove burner higher to raise the temperature, or add ice to the cold water bath to bring the temperature down.

5. When both the oils and the lye mixture are at 110°F, pour the lye mixture into the plastic container with the oils. Blend with your stick blender until the mixture reaches a light trace stage, then add your fragrances. Blend until the mixture reaches medium trace (see page 26).

6. Pour into a chilled mold and refrigerate, uncovered, for 30 minutes. Remove from the refrigerator; spray the top with isopropyl alcohol, cover loosely with plastic wrap, and refrigerate overnight.

7. Remove from refrigerator and let sit at room temperature.

8. Unmold 24 hours after pouring into the mold. Cut into bars, spritz with isopropyl alcohol, and place in your curing area.

CUT GRASS SOAP

mix temp
90°F

This bar will make you think of summer. Lying in a hammock, dozing, the scent of a freshly mowed lawn wafting in the air.... You could even pretend that the gardener mowed the lawn, not you!

OILS

170 grams shea butter

170 grams palm oil

113 grams coconut oil

113 grams peppermint-infused olive oil (see directions below)

LYE MIXTURE

78 grams sodium hydroxide (NaOH)

215 grams chilled coconut milk

ADD AT TRACE

34 grams grass stain fragrance oil

¼ teaspoon peppermint leaves (from the strained oil infusion)

1. Measure your fragrance into a small glass container, add the ¼ teaspoon peppermint leaves, and set aside.

   Measure the oils into a plastic container. Place the container in a larger pot and pour in enough hot tap water that the container begins to float. Set the pot on the stove and turn the heat to warm. Insert a thermometer into the oils.

2. Goggles and gloves on!

3. Measure the chilled coconut milk into a heat-safe glass container; set the container in an ice water bath. Measure the lye crystals into a separate small glass container. Slowly add the lye crystals to the coconut milk, stirring with your spatula as you do so. Insert a thermometer into the lye mixture.

The purée will darken in color and thicken; keep stirring. If you notice the temperature rising above 140°F, add more ice to your cold water bath. Do not inhale above this container!

4. Monitor the temperatures of the two containers. You want both containers to reach 90°F. As needed, refresh the hot water bath or turn the stove burner higher to raise the temperature, or add ice to the cold water bath to bring the temperature down.

5. When both the oils and the lye mixture are at 90°F, pour the lye mixture into the plastic container with the oils. Blend with your stick blender until the mixture reaches a light trace stage, then add the fragrance–tea leaf mixture. Blend until the mixture reaches medium trace (see page 26).

6. Pour into a chilled mold and refrigerate, uncovered, for 30 minutes. Remove from the refrigerator; spray the top with isopropyl alcohol, cover loosely with plastic wrap, and refrigerate overnight.

7. Remove from refrigerator and let sit at room temperature.

8. Unmold 24 hours after pouring into the mold. Cut into bars, spritz with isopropyl alcohol, and place in your curing area.

PEPPERMINT-INFUSED OLIVE OIL: In a small slow cooker set on high, heat 200 grams olive oil with the leaves from 3 peppermint tea bags. Heat for 3 hours or longer and then strain with a fine strainer. Save some of the strained leaves to add later.

If you don't have a slow cooker, warm the olive oil and peppermint tea leaves in a covered heat-proof container set in a saucepan of hot tap water. Either heat on the stove top on warm for several hours, or simply keep refreshing the hot water as it cools (this method will take longer).

HEAD-TO-TOE SHAMPOO BAR

mix temp
90°F

A shampoo bar is great for many reasons: It's a total body cleanser, it's portable for travel, and it means there's one less bottle to fall on your foot in the shower. I do still recommend using a conditioner.

Lather the bar in your hands and smooth the lather from the roots to the ends of your hair. This will minimize tangling. A shampoo bar will raise the cuticles of the hair, so I suggest using a vinegar rinse made with 1 part apple cider vinegar to 9 parts water.

OILS

142 grams castor oil

142 grams coconut oil

142 grams palm oil

85 grams olive oil

57 grams shea butter

LYE MIXTURE

79 grams sodium hydroxide (NaOH)

215 grams chilled coconut milk

ADD AT TRACE

17 grams ocean rain fragrance oil

1. Measure your fragrance into a small glass container and set aside.

   Measure the oils into a plastic container. Place the container in a larger pot and pour in enough hot tap water that the container begins to float. Set the pot on the stove and turn the heat to warm. Insert a thermometer into the oils.

2. Goggles and gloves on!

3. Measure the chilled coconut milk into a heat-safe glass container; set the container into an ice water bath. Measure the lye crystals into a separate small glass container. Slowly add the lye crystals to the coconut milk, stirring with your spatula as you do so. Insert a thermometer into the lye mixture.

The coconut milk will darken in color and thicken; keep stirring. If you notice the temperature rising above 140°F, add more ice to the cold water bath. Do not inhale above this container!

4. Monitor the temperatures of the two containers. You want both to reach 90°F. As needed, refresh the hot water bath or turn the stove burner higher to raise the temperature, or add ice to the cold water bath to bring the temperature down.

5. When both the oils and the lye mixture are at 90°F, pour the lye mixture into the plastic container with the oils. Blend with your stick blender until the mixture reaches a light trace stage, then add your fragrance. Blend until the mixture reaches medium trace (see page 26).

6. Pour into a chilled mold and refrigerate, uncovered, for 30 minutes. Remove from the refrigerator; spray the top with isopropyl alcohol, cover loosely with plastic wrap, and refrigerate overnight.

7. Remove from refrigerator and let sit at room temperature.

8. Unmold 24 hours after pouring into the mold. Cut into bars, spritz with isopropyl alcohol, and place in your curing area.

CUCUMBER MELON SOAP

mix temp
110°F

You really can't miss with this bar. People who are fussy about scents usually like cucumber melon. It's pretty much a soap staple. FYI—real cucumbers are harmed in the making of this soap. The cucumber peel imparts a lovely pale green to the finished bar.

OILS

170 grams shea butter

170 grams palm oil

113 grams coconut oil

113 grams olive oil

LYE MIXTURE

78 grams sodium hydroxide (NaOH)

215 grams chilled cucumber–coconut milk purée (see directions below)

ADD AT TRACE

34 grams cucumber-melon fragrance oil

1. Measure your fragrance into a small glass container and set aside.

   Measure the oils into a plastic container. Place the container in a larger pot and pour in enough hot tap water that the container begins to float. Set the pot on the stove and turn the heat to warm. Insert a thermometer into the oils.

2. Goggles and gloves on!

3. Measure the your chilled cucumber–coconut milk purée into a heat-safe glass container; place the container in an ice water bath. Measure the lye crystals into a separate small glass container. Slowly add the lye crystals to the cucumber–coconut milk purée, stirring with your spatula as you do so. Insert a thermometer into the mixture.

The purée will darken in color and thicken; keep stirring. If you notice the temperature rising above 140°F, add more ice to your cold water bath. Do not inhale above this container!

4. Monitor the temperatures of the two containers. You want both to reach 110°F. As needed, refresh the hot water bath or turn the stove burner higher to raise the temperature, or add ice to the cold water bath to bring the temperature down.

5. When both the oils and the lye mixture are at 110°F, pour the lye mixture into the plastic container with the oils. Blend with your stick blender until the mixture reaches a light trace stage, then add your fragrance. Blend until the mixture reaches medium trace (see page 26).

6. Pour into a chilled mold and refrigerate, uncovered, for 30 minutes. Remove from the refrigerator; spray the top with isopropyl alcohol, cover loosely with plastic wrap, and refrigerate overnight.

7. Remove from refrigerator and let sit at room temperature.

8. Unmold 24 hours after pouring into the mold. Cut into bars, spritz with isopropyl alcohol, and place in your curing area.

CUCUMBER–COCONUT MILK PURÉE: Using a blender, purée 100 grams coconut milk with 150 grams English cucumber, including peel. (English cucumbers have smaller seeds than other types. Regular cucumbers can be used, but seed them first.) Purée until all lumps are gone. Small flecks of peel will remain.

CRANBERRY POMEGRANATE SOAP

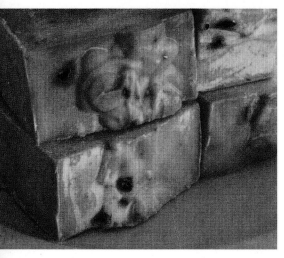

mix temp
110°F

This is one of those scents that some of us can't really seem to get enough of. I'll have a bar out, curing, and I'll notice that I'm picking it up to smell it every time I walk by. Its sweet and tart scent is just delicious.

OILS

170 grams shea butter

170 grams palm oil

113 grams coconut oil

113 grams olive oil

LYE MIXTURE

78 grams sodium hydroxide (NaOH)

215 grams chilled coconut milk

1 tablespoon chopped dried cranberries

ADD AT TRACE

34 grams cranberry-pomegranate fragrance oil

1 teaspoon chopped dried cranberries (from strained purée)

1. Using a blender, purée the coconut milk with the 1 tablespoon chopped dried cranberries. Strain, saving both the purée and berries left in the strainer. Measure your fragrance into a small glass container, add 1 teaspoon of the chopped dried cranberries from the strained purée, and set aside.

   Measure the oils into a plastic container. Place the container in a larger pot and pour in enough hot tap water that the container begins to float. Set the pot on the stove and turn the heat to warm. Insert a thermometer into the oils.

2. Goggles and gloves on!

3. Measure the chilled coconut milk into a heat-safe glass container; place the container in an ice water bath. Measure the lye crystals into a separate small glass container. Slowly add the lye crystals to the coconut

milk, stirring with your spatula as you do so. Insert a thermometer into the mixture.

The purée will darken in color and thicken; keep stirring. If you notice the temperature rising above 140°F, add more ice to your cold water bath. Do not inhale above this container!

4. Monitor the temperatures of the two containers. You want both to reach 110°F. As needed, refresh the hot water bath or turn the stove burner higher to raise the temperature, or add ice to the cold water bath to bring the temperature down.

5. When both the oils and the lye mixture are at 110°F, pour the lye mixture into the plastic container with the oils. Blend with your stick blender until the mixture reaches a light trace stage, then add your fragrance-cranberry mixture. Blend until the mixture reaches medium trace (see page 26).

6. Pour into your chilled mold. Use tiny pieces of dried cranberry to decorate the top. Spray with isopropyl alcohol, cover loosely with plastic wrap, and refrigerate overnight.

7. Remove from refrigerator and let sit at room temperature.

8. Unmold 24 hours after pouring into the mold. Cut into bars, spritz with isopropyl alcohol, and place in your curing area.

PUMPKIN SPICE SOAP

mix temp **110°F** *Pumpkin pie reminds me of Thanksgiving, being with family and friends, feeling safe and loved—and this great fall soap smells just like pumpkin pie. Since pumpkin pie is a comfort food, I guess this is a comfort soap! I know someone who gave a bar to each of her Thanksgiving dinner guests. They loved it!*

OILS

170 grams shea butter

170 grams palm oil

113 grams coconut oil

113 grams olive oil

LYE MIXTURE

78 grams sodium hydroxide (NaOH)

150 grams canned pumpkin (pure pumpkin purée, not pumpkin pie filling)

65 grams distilled water

ADD AT TRACE

30 grams pumpkin spice fragrance oil

½ teaspoon pumpkin pie spice

1. Measure your fragrance into a small glass container, add the pumpkin pie spice, and set aside.

   Measure the oils into a plastic container. Place the container in a larger pot and pour in enough hot tap water that the container begins to float. Set the pot on the stove and turn the heat to warm. Insert a thermometer into the oils.

2. Goggles and gloves on!

3. Measure the pumpkin into a heat-safe glass container; place the container in an ice water bath. Measure the distilled water into another heat-safe glass container. Measure the lye crystals into a separate small glass container.

Slowly add the lye crystals to the distilled water, making sure all the crystals dissolve. (It's hard to see whether the crystals are dissolved if you add them directly to the pumpkin, so we do it this way to make sure there are no chunks.) Now add this mixture to the pumpkin purée, stirring with your spatula as you do so. Insert a thermometer into the mixture.

The purée will darken in color and thicken; keep stirring. If you notice the temperature rising above 140°F, add more ice to the cold water bath. Do not inhale above this container!

4. Monitor the temperatures of the two containers. You want both to reach 110°F. As needed, refresh the hot water bath or turn the stove burner higher to raise the temperature, or add ice to the cold water bath to bring the temperature down.

5. When both the oils and the lye mixture are at 110°F, pour the lye mixture into the plastic container with the oils. Blend with your stick blender until the mixture reaches a light trace stage, then add your fragrance-spice mixture. Blend until the mixture reaches medium trace (see page 26).

6. Pour into a chilled mold and refrigerate, uncovered, for 30 minutes. Remove from the refrigerator; spray the top with isopropyl alcohol, cover loosely with plastic wrap, and refrigerate overnight.

7. Remove from refrigerator and let sit at room temperature.

8. Unmold 24 hours after pouring into the mold. Cut into bars, spritz with isopropyl alcohol, and place in your curing area.

CITRUS SOAP

mix temp
110°F

The very first scented soap I ever made, this bar has an invigorating fragrance that really wakes you up in the morning. I incorporate carrots to impart a beautiful yellow-orange color. The sugar in the carrots also adds to the lather.

OILS

170 grams shea butter

170 grams palm oil

113 grams coconut oil

113 grams olive oil

LYE MIXTURE

78 grams sodium hydroxide (NaOH)

100 grams carrot baby food

115 grams distilled water

ADD AT TRACE

30 grams energy fragrance oil

1. Using a blender, purée the carrot baby food with the distilled water; you will have 215 grams of purée. Chill.

2. Measure your fragrance into a small glass container and set aside.

   Measure the oils into a plastic container. Place the container in a larger pot and pour in enough hot tap water that the container begins to float. Set the pot on the stove and turn the heat to warm. Insert a thermometer into the oils.

3. Goggles and gloves on!

4. Transfer the chilled carrot purée to a heat-safe glass container; place the container in an ice water bath. Measure the lye crystals into a separate small glass container. Slowly add the lye crystals to the carrot purée, stirring with your spatula as you do so and making sure all the crystals dissolve. Insert a thermometer into the mixture.

The purée will darken in color and thicken; keep stirring. If you notice the temperature rising above 140°F, add more ice to your cold water bath. Do not inhale above this container!

5. Monitor the temperatures of the two containers. You want both to reach 110°F. As needed, refresh the hot water bath or turn the stove burner higher to raise the temperature, or add ice to the cold water bath to bring the temperature down.

6. When both the oils and the lye mixture are at 110°F, pour the lye mixture into the plastic container with the oils. Blend with your stick blender until the mixture reaches a light trace stage, then add your fragrance. Blend until the mixture reaches medium trace (see page 26).

7. Pour into a chilled mold and refrigerate, uncovered, for 30 minutes. Remove from the refrigerator; spray the top with isopropyl alcohol, cover loosely with plastic wrap, and refrigerate overnight.

8. Remove from refrigerator and let sit at room temperature.

9. Unmold 24 hours after pouring into the mold. Cut into bars, spritz with isopropyl alcohol, and place in your curing area.

CARROT & GINGER SOAP

mix temp
90°F

Carrot and ginger soup is popular, I figured, so why not do soap instead of soup? The sugar in the carrots makes for great lather. The ginger adds a bit of heat to help the circulation and maybe get your blood pumping. I use a crinkle cutter to cut my bars—they look great, and the crinkly surface emphasizes the fact that this soap is made from carrots.

FRAGRANCE-FREE

OILS

170 grams shea butter

170 grams palm oil

113 grams coconut oil

113 grams olive oil

LYE MIXTURE

78 grams sodium hydroxide (NaOH)

215 grams chilled puréed carrots (I use baby food)

ADD AT TRACE

1 teaspoon ground ginger (more or less, depending on personal preference)

1. Measure the ground ginger into a small glass container and set aside. (After your first batch, you may want to adjust the amount of ginger.)

   Measure the oils into a plastic container. Place the container in a larger pot and pour in enough hot tap water that the container begins to float. Set the pot on the stove and turn the heat to warm. Insert a thermometer into the oils.

2. Goggles and gloves on!

3. Measure the chilled carrot purée into a heat-safe glass container; place the container in an ice water bath. Measure the lye crystals into a separate small glass container. Slowly add the lye crystals to the carrot purée, stirring with your spatula as you do so and making sure all the crystals dissolve. Insert a thermometer into the mixture.

The purée will darken in color and thicken; keep stirring. If you notice the temperature rising above 140°F, add more ice to your cold water bath. Do not inhale above this container!

4. Monitor the temperatures of the two containers. You want both to reach 90°F. As needed, refresh the hot water bath or turn the stove burner higher to raise the temperature, or add ice to the cold water bath to bring the temperature down.

5. When both the oils and the lye mixture are at 90°F, pour the lye mixture into the plastic container with the oils. Blend with your stick blender until the mixture reaches a light trace stage, then add the ground ginger. Blend until the mixture reaches medium trace (see page 26).

6. Pour into a chilled mold and refrigerate, uncovered, for 30 minutes. Remove from the refrigerator; spray the top with isopropyl alcohol, cover loosely with plastic wrap, and refrigerate overnight.

7. Remove from refrigerator and let sit at room temperature.

8. Unmold 24 hours after pouring into the mold. Cut into bars, spritz with isopropyl alcohol, and place in your curing area.

BANANAS FOSTER SOAP

mix temp
90°F

Yes, this soap has bananas! B-A-N-A-N-A-S! Have you ever had those banana-shaped candies made by that famous candy maker Willy Wonka? This soap smells just like them. When I buy a bag of assorted flavors, my husband always eats all the banana pieces and leaves the rest. The banana ones are the best! I call this soap Bananas Foster to give it a bit of class— Banana Runts just doesn't have the same effect.

OILS

170 grams shea butter

170 grams palm oil

113 grams coconut oil

113 grams olive oil

LYE MIXTURE

78 grams sodium hydroxide (NaOH)

1 (13.5-ounce) can coconut milk

1 banana

ADD AT TRACE

34 grams monkey love fragrance oil

1. Using a blender, purée the coconut milk with the banana. Chill until ready to use.

2. Measure your fragrance into a small glass container and set aside.

   Measure the oils into to a plastic container. Place the container in a larger pot and pour in enough hot tap water that the container begins to float. Set the pot on the stove and turn the heat to warm. Insert a thermometer into the oils.

3. Goggles and gloves on!

4. Measure 215 grams of chilled coconut milk–banana purée into a heat-safe glass container; place the container in an ice water bath. Measure the lye crystals into a separate small glass container. Slowly add the lye crystals to the purée, stirring with your spatula as you do so and making sure all the crystals dissolve. Insert a thermometer into the mixture.

The purée will darken in color and thicken; keep stirring. If you notice the temperature rising above 140°F, add more ice to the cold water bath. Do not inhale above this container!

5. Monitor the temperatures of the two containers. You want both to reach 90°F. As needed, refresh the hot water bath or turn the stove burner higher to raise the temperature, or add ice to the cold water bath to bring the temperature down.

6. When both the oils and the lye mixture are at 90°F, pour the lye mixture into the plastic container with the oils. Blend with your stick blender until the mixture reaches a light trace stage, then add your fragrance. Blend until the mixture reaches medium trace (see page 26).

7. Pour into a chilled mold and refrigerate, uncovered, for about 30 minutes. Spray the top with isopropyl alcohol, cover loosely with plastic wrap, and refrigerate for 24 hours.

8. Remove from refrigerator and let sit at room temperature.

9. Unmold 24 hours after pouring into the mold. Cut into bars, spritz with isopropyl alcohol, and place in your curing area.

GEORGIA PEACH SOAP

mix temp
90°F

My dad was from Georgia. He instilled in me a love of barbecue, sweet tea, boiled peanuts, pecans (pronounced pe-CAHNS, not pee-cans), and salted watermelon. He would be glaring down on me from above if I created a peach soap and didn't name it Georgia Peach! Living in New York, I'm forced to use peaches that aren't from Georgia. This recipe calls for canned peaches for the sake of convenience, but if fresh ones are available, by all means use them!

OILS

170 grams shea butter

170 grams palm oil

113 grams coconut oil

113 grams olive oil

LYE MIXTURE

78 grams sodium hydroxide (NaOH)

215 grams chilled peach purée (see directions below)

ADD AT TRACE

34 grams peach fragrance oil

1. Measure your fragrance into a small glass container and set aside.

   Measure the oils into a plastic container. Place the container in a larger pot and pour in enough hot tap water that the container begins to float. Set the pot on the stove and turn the heat to warm. Insert a thermometer into the oils.

2. Goggles and gloves on!

3. Measure 215 grams of chilled peach purée into a heat-safe glass container; place the container in an ice water bath. Measure the lye crystals into a separate small glass container. Slowly add the lye crystals to the purée, stirring with your spatula as you do so and making sure all the crystals dissolve. Insert a thermometer into the mixture.

   The purée will darken in color and thicken; keep stirring. If you notice the temperature rising above 140°F, add more ice to the cold water bath. Do not inhale above this container!

4. Monitor the temperatures of the two containers. You want both to reach 90°F. As needed, refresh the hot water bath or turn the stove burner higher to raise the temperature, or add ice to the cold water bath to bring the temperature down.

5. When both the oils and the lye mixture are at 90°F, pour the lye mixture into the plastic container with the oils. Blend with your stick blender until the mixture reaches a light trace stage, then add your fragrance. Blend until the mixture reaches medium trace (see page 26).

6. Pour into a chilled mold and refrigerate, uncovered, for 30 minutes. Remove from the refrigerator; spray the top with isopropyl alcohol, cover loosely with plastic wrap, and refrigerate overnight.

7. Remove from refrigerator and let sit at room temperature.

8. Unmold 24 hours after pouring into the mold. Cut into bars, spritz with isopropyl alcohol, and place in your curing area.

PEACH PURÉE: Drain 2 (15-ounce) cans of sliced peaches, rinse with tap water, and purée them right in the can with a stick blender. Chill. It doesn't matter what the peaches are packed in—juice, light syrup, or heavy syrup, because you will be rinsing them.

CHAPTER 6
RECIPES TO IMPRESS

As you probably know by now, making soap isn't hard, it just takes practice. Once you have the basics down, you can start combining different recipes together to make some great-smelling soaps. The first two recipes in this chapter aren't hard to make, but the finished bars look impressive. The last recipe, Leaf Spa Bar, moves very quickly and should only be done after you are very comfortable with soap making.

VANILLA LIME SOAP MOSAIC

This recipe is made in two stages. First you make lime soap to cut into cubes, then you make vanilla soap to embed the cubes in. To make lime balls instead of cubes, simply roll the cubes into balls and let them cure for a bit. Be sure to plan ahead—the lime soap needs to cure for a couple of days.

By the time you tackle this recipe you'll likely be adept at making soap, so the instructions aren't as detailed. For a refresher on any of the steps, check Chapter 2 (page 23).

MAKES 12 TO 16 BARS, 3½ TO 4 OUNCES EACH

LIME CUBES

mix temp
110°F *This step needs to be done ahead of time. I use a 2-pound wooden mold for this part of the recipe, but any mold will do, since the loaf will be cut into cubes. This can be made as a stand-alone soap, too.*

OILS

170 grams shea butter	78 grams sodium hydroxide (NaOH)	**ADD AT TRACE**
170 grams palm oil	215 grams distilled water	30 grams lime fragrance oil
113 grams coconut oil		½ teaspoon lime zest (from about 2 limes)
113 grams olive oil		

LYE MIXTURE

1. Measure your fragrance into a small glass container, stir in the lime zest, and set aside.

   Measure the oils into a plastic container. Place the container in a larger pot and pour in enough hot tap water that the container begins to float. Set the pot on the stove and turn the heat to warm. Insert a thermometer into the oils.

2. Goggles and gloves on!

3. Measure the distilled water into a heat-safe glass container. Measure the lye crystals into a separate small glass container. Slowly add the lye crystals to the water, stirring with your spatula. Do not inhale above this container! This mixture will heat up quickly. Insert a thermometer into the mixture.

4. Bring both containers to the mixing temperature of 110°F and then pour the lye mixture into the oils. Blend with your stick blender. Once the mixture reaches a light trace, add your fragrance-zest mixture. Blend until medium trace.

5. Pour into a 2-pound mold and cover loosely with plastic wrap. Let sit for 24 hours at room temperature.

6. Unmold and cut into 1- to 1½-inch cubes. Separate the cubes into two batches, cover loosely with plastic wrap, and cure to let the color deepen. They should sit at room temperature. There is no need to spray with isopropyl alcohol.

VANILLA SOAP (EMBEDDING BASE)

mix temp **110°F** *I use two 2-pound wooden loaf molds to make the final loaves of soap— the shape makes it easy to embed the lime cubes. Have the molds lined and ready to use.*

OILS	LYE MIXTURE	ADD AT TRACE
204 grams shea butter	93 grams sodium hydroxide (NaOH)	40 grams vanilla select fragrance oil
204 grams palm oil		
136 grams coconut oil	259 grams distilled water	
136 grams olive oil		

1. Measure your fragrance into a small glass container and set aside.

   Measure the oils into a plastic container. Place the container in a larger pot and pour in enough hot tap water that the container begins to float. Set the pot on the stove and turn the heat to warm. Insert a thermometer into the oils.

2. Goggles and gloves on!

3. Measure the distilled water into a heat-safe glass container. Measure the lye crystals into a separate small glass container. Slowly add the lye crystals to the water, stirring with your spatula. Do not inhale above this

container! This mixture will heat up quickly. Insert a thermometer into the mixture.

4. When both the oils and the lye mixture are at 110°F, pour the lye mixture into the oils. Blend with your stick blender until the mixture reaches a light trace, then blend in your fragrance completely. Your mixture needs to be a light to medium trace. Don't let it get too thick!

5. Pour vanilla base into the molds to just cover the bottom. Start adding lime cubes. I usually alternate loaves, adding a cube to one and then to the other, to keep things even. Push the cubes gently into the vanilla. Add more vanilla base as needed. It's almost like making lasagna!

   Alternate lime cubes and vanilla base until your molds are full. You can choose to have the top be just the vanilla or have some of the lime cubes poking out—this gives a nice two-color effect on the tops of the bars.

   Tap each mold on the sides and bottom to release any air bubbles. Spray with isopropyl alcohol, cover loosely with plastic wrap, and set aside for another 24 hours at room temperature. The color will look a little funny, but the vanilla will deepen to a nice brown color as it cures.

6. Unmold, cut into bars, spritz with isopropyl alcohol, and place in your curing area.

APPLE BUTTER SOAP

Here's another eye-catching soap that's made in two stages. First you make vanilla soap to be cut into cubes. Then you make apple soap as a base for embedding the vanilla chunks.

MAKES 12 TO 16 BARS, 3½ TO 4 OUNCES EACH

VANILLA CUBES

mix temp **110°F** *Prepare these soap cubes 2 days ahead; I make mine in a 2-pound mold. This recipe can also be made as a stand-alone soap.*

OILS	LYE MIXTURE	ADD AT TRACE
170 grams shea butter	78 grams sodium hydroxide (NaOH)	34 grams vanilla select fragrance oil
170 grams palm oil	215 grams distilled water	
113 grams coconut oil		
113 grams olive oil		

1. Measure your fragrance into a small glass container and set aside.

   Measure the oils into a plastic container. Place the container in a larger pot and pour in enough hot tap water that the container begins to float. Set the pot on the stove and turn the heat to warm. Insert a thermometer into the oils.

2. Goggles and gloves on!

3. Measure the distilled water into a heat-safe glass container. Measure the lye crystals into a separate small glass container. Slowly add the lye crystals to the water, stirring with your spatula. Do not inhale above this container! This mixture will heat up quickly. Insert a thermometer into the mixture.

4. When both the oils and the lye mixture reach 110°F, pour the lye mixture into the oils. Blend with your stick blender until the mixture reaches a light trace, then add the fragrance. Blend until medium trace.

5. Pour into your mold, cover loosely with plastic wrap, and let sit at room temperature.

6. Unmold 24 hours after pouring into your mold, and cut into 1- to 1½-inch cubes. Separate the cubes into two batches, cover lightly with plastic wrap, and let cure for several hours. There is no need to spray with isopropyl alcohol.

APPLE SOAP (EMBEDDING BASE)

mix temp *I use two 2-pound wooden loaf molds to make my final loaves. Have your* **110°F** *molds lined and ready to use.*

OILS	LYE MIXTURE	ADD AT TRACE
170 grams shea butter	78 grams sodium hydroxide (NaOH)	10 grams applejack peel fragrance oil
170 grams palm oil		
113 grams coconut oil	215 grams distilled water	
113 grams olive oil		

1. Measure your fragrance into a small glass container and set aside.

   Measure the oils into a plastic container. Place the container in a larger pot and pour in enough hot tap water that the container begins to float. Set the pot on the stove and turn the heat to warm. Insert a thermometer into the oils.

2. Goggles and gloves on!

3. Measure the distilled water into a heat-safe glass container. Measure the lye crystals into a separate small glass container. Slowly add the lye crystals to the water, stirring with your spatula. Do not inhale above this container! This mixture will heat up quickly. Insert a thermometer into the mixture.

4. When both the oils and the lye mixture are at 110°F, pour the lye mixture into the oils. Blend together with your stick blender until the mixture reaches a light trace, then blend in your fragrance completely. Your mixture needs to be a light to medium trace. Don't let it get too thick!

5. Pour apple base into the molds to just cover the bottom. Start adding vanilla cubes. I alternate loaves, adding a cube to one and then to the other, to keep things even. Push the cubes gently into the apple soap. Add more apple base as needed. Alternate cubes and base until your molds are full. You can have the top be just the apple soap or let some of the vanilla cubes poke out for a two-color effect on the tops of the bars.

   Tap each mold on the sides and bottom to release any air bubbles. Spray the top with isopropyl alcohol, cover loosely with plastic wrap, and set aside at room temperature for another 24 hours. The color will look a bit clashy at first, but the vanilla will deepen to a nice brown hue as the soap cures.

6. Unmold, cut into bars, spritz with isopropyl alcohol, and place in your curing area.

LEAF SPA BAR

mix temp
110°F

Looks are deceiving when it comes to the Leaf Spa Bar. This is a salt bar, but salt bars aren't scrubs—the bar will become smooth, like stone. It produces a foamy lather that softens the skin. It's like taking a dip in the ocean! I've noticed that this soap looks great when cut into chunky bars, but it's much easier to use when you cut it into eight bars instead of six. The fragrance smells like a fresh green leaf.

MAKES 6 TO 8 BARS, 4½ TO 5 OUNCES EACH

OILS

340 grams coconut oil

45 grams shea butter

45 grams palm oil

23 grams olive oil

LYE MIXTURE

62 grams sodium hydroxide (NaOH)

172 grams distilled water

ADD AT TRACE

27 grams lettuce fragrance oil

453 grams kosher salt or sea salt

1. Measure your fragrance into a small glass container and set aside. Measure the salt into a separate container and set aside.

   Measure the oils into a plastic container. Place the container in a larger pot and pour in enough hot tap water that the container begins to float. Set the pot on the stove and turn the heat to warm. Insert a thermometer into the oils.

2. Goggles and gloves on!

3. Measure the distilled water into a heat-safe glass container. Measure the lye crystals into a separate small glass container. Slowly add the lye crystals to the water, stirring with your spatula. Do not inhale above this container! This mixture will heat up quickly. Insert a thermometer into the mixture.

4. Monitor the temperatures of the two containers. You want both to reach 110°F. When both the oils and the lye mixture are at 110°F, pour the

lye mixture into the oils. Blend with your stick blender until the mixture reaches a very light trace. Add your fragrance and blend for just a few pulses. Stir in the salt with your spatula. This will be very thick! Mix well.

5. Scoop the soap into your chilled mold, sprinkle the top with just a bit of coarse sea salt for decoration, if desired, and cover loosely with plastic wrap. Unmold when the soap is cool enough to handle—this usually only takes a couple of hours at room temperature, maybe even less.

6. Cut as soon as you unmold. If you let the soap set for too long, your bars will break when you try to cut them. Place in your curing area.

PACKAGING & PRESENTATION

There are many easy ways to make your soap look great. Whatever kind of packaging you choose, make sure that the bar isn't completely covered—cold process soap needs to breathe. People love to be able to see and smell the soap, too.

For a simple presentation, tie a few bars together with raffia string and finish with a pretty bow. Hang a card or label from the string telling what kind of soap it is and listing the ingredients.

Here are some other easy packaging ideas.

Cigar band labels

I make my labels using a word processing program, but you can also write them by hand. A sheet of 8½ x 11-inch card stock will make 5 or 6 cigar

bands. Decorative paper would also look nice.

Cut strips 8½ x 2 inches and wrap them around the middle of the bar; glue the end down with rubber cement. A double coat of cement makes the seal more secure. Put rubber cement on the underside of the end, but also on top of your label that will cover this end.

Don't attach the labels until your soap has cured for a few weeks. Soap shrinks as it cures, and you don't want your labels to be loose.

Tea bags

I used this packaging idea at Christmastime to make stocking stuffers. Just make sure to tell people that it isn't really tea, and that they do have to remove the paper to use it!

To wrap a small, rectangular piece of soap, start with a strip of tissue paper 2½ times the soap's long side in width, about 10 times that in length. Lay your soap in the center (picture 1). Fold the tissue over the soap, tape, and pleat both sides (picture 2).

Fold one side over, leaving the soap lying flat. Snip off the excess, leaving tissue paper about double the height of your bar (picture 3). Fold one corner then the other corner. Fold the top point down (picture 4). Place a long piece of string on the fold and staple the fold closed (picture 5). Tie the string ends in a knot about 7 inches from the tea bag. Staple the string to a little square label, using the knot as an anchor to secure the string (picture 6). It's your finished tea bag soap!

picture 1   picture 2

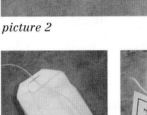

picture 3   picture 4   picture 5   picture 6

Tissue paper with sticky labels

A really easy way to package soap is to wrap it in tissue paper and use a sticky label to secure each end. I wrap my small round shaving bars this way. I roll the soap on its side in a strip of tissue paper, leaving it open at top and bottom. I then fold pleats to cover the top and bottom and seal them with the labels. It's sort of like gift-wrapping a drum, or a popcorn tin!

The label on the top tells what kind of soap it is, and the bottom label lists the ingredients. This packaging can be used on soap that hasn't fully cured, because the tissue paper lets the soap breathe.

APPENDIX

Glossary of Soap-Making Terms

Carrier oil—An oil used to dilute essential oils or fragrance oils. It "carries" the fragrance and acts as a base for ingredients that shouldn't be applied directly to the skin.

Dedicate to soap (DTS)—Equipment used in soap making that shouldn't then be used for other kitchen tasks. I actually write DTS with a Sharpie on the items in question.

Embeds—Ingredients that you put into your soap at the pouring stage. These could be other types of soap, herbs, or anything that's heat resistant and will be okay getting wet.

Essential oil—A rapidly evaporating oil that retains the scent, flavor, and other characteristic properties of the plant from which it is obtained.

Exfoliants—Ingredients added to soap that help remove dead skin cells.

False trace—When a soap mixture's temperature falls below the melting point of any of the solid oils being used, causing the mixture to thicken as if it has reached trace—though it really hasn't.

Fragrance calculator—A tool used to determine how much fragrance is needed for a given oil weight.

Fragrance oil—A blended synthetic aroma compound or essential oil that has been diluted with a carrier oil.

Gel stage—When heat generated by the chemical reaction of saponification gets high enough to cause soap to almost liquefy and turn translucent. Some soap makers insulate their molds to encourage this, creating a somewhat translucent bar that cures faster. However, it can also cause cracking and uneven color.

Glycerin—A clear, thick liquid that is a by-product of cold process soap making. A humectant, glycerin is used in many soaps and lotions to moisturize.

Heavy trace—When the soap mixture has a very thick texture, like pudding. This can be very hard to get into your mold and should be avoided.

Humectant—A substance that absorbs water from the air and helps other substances retain moisture.

Infusion—The process of extracting certain properties from a substance by steeping it in oil or water.

Light trace—When the soap mixture has the texture of pancake batter and when drizzled it leaves thin trails that sink back into the rest of the mixture.

Lye—NaOH, sodium hydroxide; the catalyst for saponification.

Lye calculator—A tool used to determine how much lye is needed to turn different oils into soaps.

Medium trace—When the soap mixture has the texture of a thick gravy and when drizzled it leaves trails on top that don't sink back into the rest of the mixture.

NaOH—Sodium hydroxide, the chemical name for the most common form of lye.

Saponification—The chemical reaction in which sodium hydroxide (lye), an alkali, meets a fatty acid (oil), splitting the oil into a fatty acid and glycerin. The sodium joins with the fatty acid to form a sodium salt—soap.

Sodium hydroxide—NaOH, the most common form of lye.

Superfatting—Using a little more oil than the required 1:1 ratio of oil to lye. This leaves a bit of unreacted oil in soap and makes for a moisturizing bar. It also assures that the bar won't be lye-heavy.

Tare—A function on a scale that resets the display to zero when there is weight on the scale. This lets you weigh your ingredients and not the container.

Trace—The thickening of the soap mixture that occurs when saponification begins, called "trace" because soap mixture drizzled across the top will leave trails, or traces. See also "Light trace," "Medium trace," and "Heavy trace."

Resources

The soap-making materials used in this book can be ordered from **Bramble Berry** at www.brambleberry.com (2138 Humboldt Street, Bellingham, WA 98225; phone 360-734-8278, fax 360-752-0992).

My recipes were designed using the **SoapCalc Lye Calculator**, available at www.soapcalc.net.

Tractor Supply Co. (www.tractorsupply.com) was my source for the lye used in these soaps.

The Red Raspberry Tea and Indian Spice Tea used in some of the soap recipes are from **Harney & Sons Fine Teas** (www.harney.com).

Conversions

MEASURE	EQUIVALENT	METRIC
1 teaspoon	--	5 milliliters
1 tablespoon	3 teaspoons	14.8 milliliters
1 cup	16 tablespoons	236.8 milliliters
1 pint	2 cups	473.6 milliliters
1 quart	4 cups	947.2 milliliters
1 liter	4 cups + 3½ tablespoons	1000 milliliters
1 ounce (dry)	2 tablespoons	28.35 grams
1 pound	16 ounces	453.49 grams
2.21 pounds	35.3 ounces	1 kilogram
90°F/110°F/140°F	--	32°C/43°C/60°C

ACKNOWLEDGMENTS

I want to thank my family for putting up with a house that has been over-run with soap, for being my guinea pigs for each and every new recipe, for basically letting me do what I had to do in order for all this to come together. I love you guys! I also want to thank my coworkers for encouraging me to write this book and having the faith that I could. Last, but not least, I would like to thank my mom for always believing in me, indulging my every creative whim as a child, and being my biggest cheerleader. I love you, Mom!

ABOUT THE AUTHOR

HEIDI CORLEY BARTO is a graduate of the School of Visual Arts in New York City. She lives in Wingdale, New York, with her husband, Rick, daughters, Gillian and Paige, along with their Vizsla, Penelope. Unable to find soap that did not irritate her youngest daughter's skin, she started creating her own, and her soap-making business Penelope B. Soap was born. When not making soap, she is the Assistant to the Director at her local library where she helps the public find books to read, helps the tech un-savvy navigate the Web, sees books on awesome hobbies she wants to try, and basically troubleshoots all day long. This is her first book.